OMG. That's Paleo?

Juli Bauer

Published by Scribe Publishing Company
Royal Oak, Michigan
www.scribe-publishing.com

Copyright © 2013 by Juli Bauer
Design by Hadrout Advertising + Technology
Cover photography by Ian Wittenber

ISBN 978-0-9859562-4-0

Library of Congress Control Number: 2012956068

Printed in the U.S.

Table of Contents

Thank You

PaleOMG Readers – I would not be writing a cookbook if it weren't for all of you. Thank you for eating paleo, for loving food as much as I do, and for inspiring me to create a cookbook to share with even more food lovers.

Mom and Dad – Thank you for every single thing you have done for me. You have no idea what your support has done for me. I know I sometimes suck as a daughter, but I at least hope to make you proud with this cookbook.

Laura Hazlett – Thank you for trying all my recipes, giving me feedback, and supporting me, even when I stayed in on Friday and Saturday nights to blog. You're the best friend a person could ask for.

Sergio Nazarro – Thank you for helping me stay true to myself and being proud of me no matter what. Sometimes I need reminding that I'm an only child.

Jason and Jake and everyone at CrossFit Broadway – You are my second home and my second family. Thank you for supporting me from the very start... even if you do secretly hate my blog. Okay, not so secretly whatsoever.

Ian Wittenber – You're amazing. If it weren't for you, I wouldn't have this awesome cookbook cover. It's hard work to make me look decent on film, so I appreciate your time and patience throughout our photo shoot.

Jon Moffitt – Thank you for introducing me to CrossFit, starting paleo with me, and spending many late nights in the bulk isle at Whole Foods with me. Sampling. Mostly things covered in chocolate.

Tom Ashby and Renegade Fitness – Thank you for believing in me and helping me grow my brand with my videos and apparel. You're awesome, Tom.

Kevin Montoya – Thank you for helping me start my CrossFit and paleo journey. Every opportunity you have given me has led me to where I am now.

Peter Schmalfeldt – Thank you for creating the website I have today and helping me share my recipes all over the world. All of this would not be possible without your creative eye, amazing design, and crazy-intelligent brain.

Jennifer Baum, my publisher – If it weren't for you, this new chapter in my life would not be happening. This book is because of you and I can't show you my appreciation enough.

CrossFit Evolve – You were my first CrossFit home. Thank you for posting my recipes on your website and sharing them with your friends and family.

Everyone at Again Faster – Thank you for believing in me. Your support in my writing, my cooking abilities, and my competitions has helped me build more confidence than I knew I had.

Rj Smith – Thank you for letting me use your kitchen so many times for cooking videos AND the cookbook photo shoot. If you didn't have the nicest kitchen of all my friends, I would have had to film in an elementary school kitchen, and you know how much I like kids.

Jameson and Tony's Market – Thank you for the donation of seafood. Without your shrimp and scallops, my seafood lovers would go hungry.

About JB:

Here are some things you should know about me. I sometimes talk about myself in the third person. I have a self-given nickname. And I spend most of my days obsessing about what my next meal will be. I'm a paleo blogger, a Level 1 CrossFit coach and athlete, and a food hoarder. I love coffee. I hate olives. And I can eat my body weight in nut butter. Trust me, it's impressive. Especially since I'm pretty much allergic to nuts. That's fun.

I grew up loving food. I remember coming home from school and making myself chocolate chip pancakes... Every. Day. I also remember spending my days with constant stomach aches, trips to the emergency room because I could barely walk from the aches, and being in a constant battle with food. Food was often my best friend, but more so my enemy. I hated what food did to my body. I didn't understand what food was made for: to nourish us. It wasn't until I found paleo that food officially became my one true love. I began to figure out what foods worked for my body, began eating foods I never thought I would try, and began sharing my love for food with the world through my blog: paleomg.com.

Here's the thing. I don't claim to know all the science behind paleo, and in all honesty, I don't care. I just know how I feel. I know that since I started eating paleo, my stomach issues have gone away. I know that I haven't been sick in two years. And I know that any sort of depression I had pre-paleo has disappeared. I have created my own version of paleo and have figured out what works for me and my body. My version of paleo includes dark chocolate and bacon. I know, I know, my life does sound pretty great, doesn't it? But eating paleo has given me the tools to create a lifestyle I can stick with and enjoy, because I know exactly what works for my body and what doesn't.

About the blog:

My food blog is called paleomg.com. I'll help you sound it out. It confuses people. Pay-lee-O.M.G. Good work. I share my life story on that thing. It's pretty much like reading a teenage diary, but with more of a sailor-mouth. And no fun dating life.

I started my blog to share with friends what I was cooking up while trying to stick with the paleo diet.   As I began to blog more, I started to share every detail of my life throughout every post, from my love for exercise, to dating, to battles with acne, to body issues. Anything and everything goes into my blog. The more my blog grows and the more people I reach, the more I fall in love with blogging. Creating delicious food and laughter around the world is what I hope to do through my blog.

About the cookbook:

I have written this cookbook for every single PaleOMG fan that has supported me, tried a recipe, or told the world that paleo can be delicious. This cookbook is an expression of me. It has around seventy of my favorite blog recipes, as well as over thirty new ones that have never been posted on my website. Exciting!! It also has MANY pictures of me in it. I know, very self-centered. But that's what my blog is all about. Me. So if you walk away feeling like you hung out with me in your kitchen or drank a mimosa with me on your couch, good. That's exactly what I was hoping for.

I'm going to put it out there right now. I am NOT a photographer. And, I am NOT a professional chef. I am a 24-year-old woman who loves paleo food, trying new ingredients and sharing those thrown-together ingredients with the world.

And here is a disclaimer: I do curse. Not in my cookbook as much as I do in real life, or even my blog, but there is definitely some in here. It's not intended to offend you; it's simply in here because it's how I talk. Remember, I'm 24—well, turning 25 shortly after this book is released. And as much as my mother hates it, I am who I am. Curse words and all.

Okay wait, what the hell does paleo even mean?

A while back, like 2.5 million years ago (you know, when our great grandmas were still alive... that's a joke), our ancestors began to wander the earth. Like us modern humans, our hunter-gatherer ancestors had needs. And since they hadn't quite figured out how to put in cell phone towers, their main needs were eating and shelter. Back in this Paleolithic Era, our ancestors would hunt for their protein and gather for their carbohydrates and fat. They knew a well-rounded diet was important. Not really. But they did know they had to eat. Eating = energy. And energy = survival.

Problem is, since the Industrial Revolution, we have begun to consume different foods than ever before, such as refined sugars and grains, diet sodas, and poor-quality meats, in turn decreasing the quality of our own lives without even knowing it. We have more diseases than ever, and sometimes it's because of what we are putting in our bodies.

So if we go back to our roots, back to the days before fast food was around every corner, we can find foods that are pure and exactly what our bodies want, foods that nourish our bodies and fuel our fires. We need food to help us thrive, and the paleo diet will do just that. If you're ready to feel like a new person, to feel satisfied, and to be able to finally stick with a diet, the paleo diet is for you. Because it's not really a diet; it's a lifestyle. A sustainable one.

But more importantly, let's talk about JB's viewpoint on paleo:

Okay. I don't really like talking about paleo with people. I definitely like talking about food, that's for sure, but paleo... that's a touchy subject, even with people who eat paleo. Everyone thinks his or her opinion is right. Little do they know, it's actually me who is ALWAYS right. Okay, I'm kidding.

But people don't like being questioned, ESPE-CIALLY if it's about what they eat. So I don't question people. But when they question ME and tell ME what I'm eating is dumb, I get a bit peeved. But seriously, I don't question your oatmeal, I don't care about your pizza, and I sure don't give a sh*t about how many beers you had last night. So why do you care what I eat? Your life is YOURS. You make it whatever you want. You create your future. And you are in control of your health. So if oatmeal allows you to poop because of its 'added fiber,' well, you're a liar, but I'm happy for you.

The thing is, the pao diet was created off of what is assumed to be the caveman diet. Cool. I'm not a cave-man. I may not shower as often as I should, but I'm defi-nitely not hunting down my food, suffocating it with my massive thighs, then eating its liver for extra iron. That's just not me. Now chasing after a cupcake truck, that's a different story. But I eat a certain way because it makes me feel better. My bowel movements are awesome. Yes, I did just say that. And I perform in the gym better than I ever have. Do I eat bacon? Yes. Do I eat a CRAP TON of fat in the form of coconut butter? Sometimes, yes. Do I eat paleo baked goods far too often? Oh hell yes. But I still call myself paleo and am quite fine with that. Does that mean I follow the 'paleo guidelines' out there? No. But that's because I was crazy strict paleo for some time and it didn't work with my lifestyle. It made me crazy. Tell me I can't have something, and I want it 10 times more. I'm like any other human out there.

But because of how much I've played around with my diet, I know what works for me. I know that I can't eat a ton of cheese, but I'll definitely do it sometimes. I know my face will break out if I eat a ton of nut butters, but I'll still have a little sometimes. And I know all this stuff be-cause I've tried it all. I've eaten the Standard American Diet (and it's called S.A.D. for a reason). I've tried to eat like a vegetarian. And honestly, it wasn't until I took the paleo plunge that I felt normal. My body felt like it was working how it was supposed to.

Okay, now I'm just going on a rant. The whole rea-son I'm writing this is because paleo is what you make it. This cookbook was created to give you options. That may mean I will call my Bacon Alfredo a "paleo" dish or my coconut and almond flour waffle a "paleo" dish. You're not cool with that? You havin' a sh*t fit because cavemen didn't have the means to cook like that? Well, I don't care. Seriously. This is my cookbook and my website and I will make whatever I please and call it whatever I want.

I really do respect everyone's opinion out there, but I also never want anyone to be afraid of trying the paleo lifestyle because they think it is intimidating and/ or restricting. Try eating paleo. Try some of the recipes out there as well as those in my cookbook. And try mak-ing the paleo diet a diet that works for you.

Now that you know what my opinion is on paleo food, let's talk about what your new, delicious foods consist of!

HAPPY FOOD 101:

Lean Meats | Vegetables | Fruits | Nuts and Seeds | Healthy Fats

Get to eating your protein!!
The leaner the meats, the better for you they are. But don't be afraid of eating those fattier meats sometimes. Meat will make you feel satisfied and keep your body running how it's supposed to.

Now eat your fruits and veggies!
Any kind, any flavor, any color. The more vegetables you can eat, the better. Fruits and veggies are full of vitamins and minerals that help our bodies function optimally.

Don't be afraid of fat!
It's good for you and will make you feel satisfied with your meal. Healthy fats that are rich in Omega-3s will keep your body moving and make you feel great!

That all sounds easy to me... what am I not allowed to eat?

NAUGHTY FOOD 101:

Grains | Dairy | Legumes | Processed Foods and Sugars | Starches | Alcohol

Get rid of those grains!
For reals, throw out all the grains or grain-like foods in your house. They are bad for you. And make you sick. If you want to find out why, read a book by Robb Wolf. He explains it better than anyone I know. Even though I don't really know him.

Remove the dairy. Yes that means even your coffee creamer. I know, sad day.
Some people still eat dairy while eating paleo, which is awesome. But when you're starting off, I always recommend removing it from your diet to see if it bugs you when you eat it again.

What the hell is a legume?
It's almost anything in a pod, such as a bean or a peanut. Get rid of them. Your bum will thank you.

And throw out all of those refined and processed foods!
OMG read your labels people. If you can't pronounce the word after sounding it out three or four times, you probably shouldn't be eating it!! Go with simple foods with no added junk. You'll feel instantly better.

That was boring. Let's talk about the tools to make you a paleo pro. Remember: a paleo-prepared kitchen is a happy kitchen!

Knives – Invest in some sharp knives. All sizes. It will help. I know; I lack those in my kitchen.

Food processor – They tend to be expensive, but TOTALLY worth it. It's the kitchen device I use the most. We have a beautiful relationship. We really never fight. Best boyfriend EVER!

Slow cooker – You want simple meals? Get this. Your life will be easier than ever.

Some skillets and saucepans – All different sizes. Nonstick is always helpful.

Cutting boards – I hear wood cutting boards are supposed to be the best and healthiest option for us. I have no clue. I just like my wooden one. Mostly because it has my blog name on it.

Mandolin – Not necessary, but very helpful.

Glass baking dishes – 8x8 and 9x12 are perfect sizes to have around.

Baking sheets

Bread pans

Muffin tin

Mixing bowls

Measuring cups – I hate measuring, but baked goods come out much better when you measure.

Rubber spatula

Tongs – Rubber ones are great so you can use them in your pans. I love my tongs.

Can opener – Because our teeth just aren't strong enough sometimes.

Zester – Not necessary, but very helpful.

Parchment paper

Twine

Meat thermometer

Now what about food? No point in having the tools if you don't have the food. So I'll give you a sneak peek into what my kitchen looks like.

In the fridge:

eggs

any meat that looks good (I keep a ton in the freezer, as well)

bacon

In my produce drawer:

lemons & limes

mushrooms

green onions

cilantro

some sort of leafy green

carrots

celery

avocados

cauliflower

broccoli

fruit that's on sale

basil

sweet potatoes

onions

any squash in season

Condiments:

mustard (Dijon and yellow)

roasted red peppers in a jar

hot sauce

Sriracha

pickles

rendered bacon fat (I keep it in a jar)

duck fat (because it's awesome)

chicken broth

vegetable broth

In my spice drawer:

garlic powder

onion powder

cumin

coriander

oregano

red pepper flakes

yellow curry powder

chili powder

smoked paprika

powdered ginger

cayenne pepper

celery salt

baking soda

baking powder

cinnamon

nutmeg

cloves

garlic cloves

In my oil and vinegar cabinet (which is covered in honey and olive oil. I tend to not be very good at screwing on the caps):

extra virgin olive oil

coconut oil

walnut oil

almond oil

avocado oil

coconut aminos

balsamic vinegar

apple cider vinegar

red and/or white wine vinegar

sesame oil

In my dessert area (yes, I have a dessert area):

dark chocolate chips

unsweetened shredded coconut

coconut butter

nuts

canned coconut milk

almond flour

coconut flour

raw honey (because it's my favorite and I think it tastes the best)

vanilla extract

other extracts (coconut and maple are in there right now)

unsweetened cocoa powder

Poultry

HERE'S THE KEY TO LEARNING TO LOVE TO COOK:

1. Put on an outfit that you would rarely wear in public, let alone while cooking.

2. Pour yourself a mimosa. No, they're not paleo. But we gotta live a little sometimes, right?

3. Stuff a date with almond butter. No, not a man, (even though that may be a way to keep a man coming back) but the dried fruit kind.

4. Then consume your almond-butter-stuffed dates while dancing around the kitchen with your eyes closed. Make sure knives are put away.

If that doesn't make you love cooking or at least make you smile, I don't know what to tell you.

Okay, I'll tell you where to start if that way is not for you. Start with chicken or turkey. They are bland, lean meats that you can dress up in a plethora of ways. I love that word. It means many... at least I think it does. You can use many different spices, and these lean meats will soak them up like sponge. A delicious sponge. And if worse comes to worst, and your poultry dish tastes like poo, you can always just eat an entire package of dates and jar of almond butter.

Been there. Done that.

HERE'S WHAT'S ON THE

Menu

for all your poultry needs:

CHICKEN BASIL MEATLOAF

BUFFALO CHICKEN AND SWEET POTATO MEATZA

CILANTRO CHICKEN NUGGETS

PUMPKIN CASHEW COCONUT CHICKEN CURRY

PISTACHIO PESTO CHICKEN PASTA

JAMBALAYA

ALOO GOBI

BACON CHICKEN ALFREDO

COCONUT GINGER MUSHROOM CHICKEN

AVOCADO CILANTRO CHICKEN SALAD

CREAMY CAJUN CHICKEN PASTA

CHICKEN WITH CILANTRO AND PLANTAIN RICE

SPICY TURKEY SLIDERS OVER AVOCADO SLAW

TURKEY-STUFFED TWICE BAKED SWEET POTATOES

Chicken Basil Meatloaf

PREP TIME: 5 MINUTES • COOK TIME: 30 MINUTES

SERVES: 6-8

- 2 pounds ground chicken
- 2 eggs, whisked
- 1 cup almond flour/meal
- 1 cup fresh basil, chopped
- 1 tablespoon garlic powder
- 1 tablespoon onion powder
- 1 teaspoon dried parsley
- salt and pepper, to taste

1. Preheat oven to 375°F.
2. Mix all ingredients for meatloaf in a bowl.
3. Place ingredients into two bread loaf pans.
4. Bake for 25-30 minutes or until there is no pink remaining in the loaf.
5. Eat!
6. OMG, that was easy.

What changes did you make?

_____

_____

_____

REAL IMPORTANT STUFF...
Kind of:

- Not into ground chicken? Understandable. Try ground turkey or ground beef instead!
- Roasted cauliflower is a perfect side dish for this meatloaf. All you need is a little salt and pepper to season it up! Simple!

Cilantro Chicken Nuggets

PREP TIME: 5 MINUTES • COOK TIME: 30 MINUTES

SERVES: 2-4

For the nuggets:
- 1 pound ground chicken or ground turkey
- 1 egg, whisked
- 1 bundle of cilantro, chopped (the more, the better!)
- 3 scallions, chopped
- 2 teaspoons sesame oil
- 1/2 cup coconut flour
- 1/4 teaspoon ginger
- salt and pepper, to taste
- 1-2 tablespoons coconut oil

For the dipping sauce:
- 1/4 cup coconut aminos
- 1/8 cup white wine vinegar
- 1 tablespoon Dijon mustard
- 1 teaspoon raw honey

1. Mix all of the nugget ingredients together: ground chicken, egg, cilantro, scallions, sesame oil, ginger, salt and pepper.

2. Heat a large skillet over medium heat and add 1-2 tablespoons of coconut oil.

3. Place the coconut flour in a shallow bowl.

4. Make "nugget-sized" balls from the nugget mixture and place each nugget in the coconut flour (being sure to only lightly dust the nuggets) then place in the skillet.

5. Press down on each nugget with a spatula to slightly flatten out each nugget. It only needs a little press.

6. Cook on both sides for 5-7 minutes or until cooked through.

7. While the nuggets cook, mix the dipping sauce ingredients together.

8. Once the nuggets are done cooking, dip the little guys in the sauce and eat those grown-up nuggets up!

What changes did you make?

_____

_____

_____

REAL IMPORTANT STUFF... *Kind of:*

- *Coconut aminos are similar to soy sauce. If you cannot find them in your local store, either purchase a gluten free soy sauce or use the World Wide Web and buy online! Easy!*
- *Be careful not to overcoat your chicken nuggets. Coconut flour can be very dry and overpowering if you use too much of it. Don't say I didn't warn you!*

INGREDIENTS

- 2 pounds ground beef
- 1 pound ground chicken
- 1 large sweet potato or yam, diced (I left the skin on)
- 1/4 cup hot sauce
- 1 tablespoon dried basil
- 1 tablespoon dried parsley
- 1 tablespoon dried oregano
- 2 teaspoons garlic powder
- 2 teaspoons onion powder
- 2 tablespoons coconut oil
- salt and pepper, to taste

Buffalo Chicken and Sweet Potato Meatza

PREP TIME: 15 MINUTES • COOK TIME: 20 MINUTES
SERVES: 4-6

1. Preheat oven to 350°F.

2. Place ground beef in a bowl along with herbs: basil, parsley, and oregano, as well as some salt and pepper. Mix well. Your hands are the best tool!

3. Add the ground beef mixture to a 9×13 glass baking dish, press down into the baking dish, and place in the oven to bake for 12-15 minutes.

4. While the ground beef bakes, place a large skillet over medium heat and add coconut oil to the pan. Once the coconut oil becomes hot, add diced yam or sweet potato.

5. Cover to help steam, and cook for about 5 minutes or so.

6. When the yam begins to soften, add the ground chicken along with garlic powder, onion powder, salt and pepper.

7. Use a wooden spoon to break up the chicken, then cover to help cook through completely.

8. When the chicken is cooked through, add hot sauce and mix thoroughly.

9. When the ground beef is done cooking, remove from the oven, add the chicken and yam/sweet potato mixture on top of the beef. Then add a bit more hot sauce to top it all off.

10. Bake for about 5 minutes.

11. Then cut and serve!

What changes did you make?

_____

_____

_____

REAL IMPORTANT STUFF... *Kind of.*

- Any hot sauce will do. Use your favorite! Just make sure there is no hidden sugar in that hot sauce of yours!
- Ground turkey could also be used instead of ground chicken.

INGREDIENTS

For the curry:

- 1 pound chicken, cut into cubes
- 2 garlic cloves, minced
- 1 red onion, sliced
- 2/3 cup canned coconut milk
- 1/2 cup pureed pumpkin
- 1/2 cup cashews
- 2-3 tablespoons curry powder
- 1 tablespoon coconut oil
- 1 teaspoon ground cumin
- 1/2 teaspoon cayenne pepper
- 1/4 teaspoon red pepper flakes
- pinch of cinnamon
- salt and pepper, to taste
- cilantro, to garnish

For the coconut rice:

- 1 head cauliflower, stem removed, roughly chopped
- 1/3 cup canned coconut milk
- 1/4 cup unsweetened shredded coconut
- 1 tablespoon coconut oil
- 1 teaspoon raw honey
- pinch of salt

Pumpkin Cashew Coconut Curry over Coconut Rice

PREP TIME: 10 MINUTES • COOK TIME: 15 MINUTES

SERVES: 4

1. "Rice" the cauliflower using the shredding attachment on your food processor.

2. Pull out a large pot, place over medium heat, add a tablespoon of coconut oil, and then add cauliflower. Add a pinch of salt, then cover to help steam, mixing occasionally to keep from sticking to the bottom.

3. Pull out a large skillet and place over medium heat. Then add a tablespoon of coconut oil.

4. Add minced garlic, then add the chicken as soon as the garlic becomes fragrant.

5. Once the chicken begins to become white on all sides, add 2/3 cup coconut milk and pureed pumpkin to the chicken and mix until the pumpkin breaks down.

6. Add sliced onions and spices to cook down.

7. Then add coconut milk, shredded coconut, honey and some salt to the coconut rice and cover to cook down. Stir occasionally to make sure it doesn't burn!

8. Let the rice cook for about 5-8 minutes until the coconut milk has evaporated and you have sticky rice.

9. When the chicken is done cooking and the curry has thickened a bit, remove from heat and add the cashews to the curry mixture.

10. Place the sticky rice in a bowl, along with curry over the top and cilantro to garnish!

{

What changes did you make?

_____

_____

_____

REAL IMPORTANT STUFF... *Kind of:*

- *Don't have a food processor? Use a cheese grater to shred your cauliflower into rice. Things might get real messy, though.*
- *No pumpkin on hand? Use a winter squash such as butternut, acorn, or even kabocha.*

Pistachio Pesto Chicken Pasta

PREP TIME: 20 MINUTES • COOK TIME: 20 MINUTES

SERVES: 3-4

- 1 medium spaghetti squash, halved, seeds and excess threads removed
- 1/2 pound chicken, sliced or cubed
- 1 cup pistachios, unsalted and shelled
- 1/2 cup basil leaves, stems removed
- 2 garlic cloves
- 1/2-1 cup olive oil
- juice of 1 lemon
- salt and pepper to taste
- handful of sundried tomatoes, sliced, to garnish

1. Preheat oven to 425°F .
2. Place spaghetti squash cut-side-down on a baking sheet and cook for 20-25 minutes or until spaghetti squash is soft to the touch. Do not overcook (it will turn to mush)!
3. While the spaghetti squash cooks, put the pistachios in a food processor and pulse until crumbled.
4. Add garlic cloves and basil, then turn food processor on.
5. While the food processor is still running, add the olive oil slowly until it is incorporated, then add the lemon juice.
6. Heat up a large skillet over medium heat and add a couple tablespoons of olive oil. Add the chicken to the skillet along with some salt and pepper and cook chicken on both sides until almost cooked through, then add the pesto to the pan.
7. Coat chicken in pesto.
8. When the spaghetti squash is done cooking and has cooled a bit, use a fork to pull the threads out of the spaghetti squash and place directly into the pesto and chicken pan.
9. Combine all together.
10. Add to a bowl, top with some leftover chopped pistachios and sundried tomatoes!

What changes did you make?

_____

_____

_____

REAL IMPORTANT STUFF... *Kind of:*

- *Want to cut down calories? Try using ¼ cup olive oil and ¼ cup vegetable broth.*
- *No pistachios on hand? Walnuts or pine nuts would be a great substitute.*

Jambalaya

PREP TIME: 10 MINUTES • COOK TIME: 15 MINUTES

SERVES: 2-3

- 2 Andouille sausage, sliced
- 2 chicken breasts, cubed
- 2 garlic cloves, minced
- 1 yellow onion, diced
- 1 green bell pepper, diced
- 1 head cauliflower, riced
- 1 (6 ounce) can tomato paste
- 1 (14 ounce) can diced tomatoes, with liquid
- 1 cup chicken broth
- 2 tablespoons olive oil
- 1 teaspoon smoked paprika
- 1 teaspoon dried oregano
- 1/2 teaspoon dried thyme
- 1/2 teaspoon dried parsley
- 1/2 teaspoon cayenne pepper
- salt and pepper, to taste

1. Get everything ready. It'll make your life simpler. Dice all the veggies then throw the cauliflower in the food processor with the shredding attachment to rice the cauliflower.
2. Heat a large pot over medium-high heat and add the olive oil. Throw in the garlic until it becomes fragrant, and then add the onion and green bell pepper to begin to cook down.
3. Once the onion becomes translucent, add the cauliflower, broth, chicken and sausage. Mix together. Cover and let cook for about 5 minutes.
4. Add the diced tomatoes, tomato paste, and spices. Stir together.
5. Cover and let cook for another 5-8 minutes or until cauliflower is tender and meats are cooked through.
6. Let sit for around 5 minutes to cool.
7. Consume!

What changes did you make?

_____

_____

_____

REAL IMPORTANT STUFF... *Kind of:*

- I don't want to toot my own horn, but I will. This recipe got 5 stars out of 30 reviews on my website. That may not sound like a lot to you, but that's pretty exciting to me!
- Got some shrimp or crawfish to add to the mix? Do it! I'm jealous already.

Aloo Gobi

PREP TIME: 10 MINUTES • COOK TIME: 15 MINUTES

SERVES: 3-4

- 1 (14 ounce) can coconut milk
- 1 head of cauliflower, leaves and stem removed, chopped in small florets
- 1 sweet potato, cubed (I didn't peel it)
- 1/2 pound chicken, cubed (I used leftover shredded chicken. Genius)
- 3 garlic cloves, minced
- 1 tablespoon coconut oil
- 2 tablespoons almond butter
- 1 tablespoon curry powder
- 2 teaspoons cumin
- 1 teaspoon coriander
- 1/2 teaspoon red pepper flakes (unless you want more intense heat)
- 1/4 teaspoon cinnamon
- 1/4 teaspoon garam masala
- salt and pepper, to taste

1. Place large pot or pan over medium heat, add coconut oil and garlic to sauté.
2. Once garlic is fragrant, add the coconut milk and spices. Let simmer for about 5 minutes.
3. While the spices are simmering, chop the veggies and chicken.
4. Place sweet potatoes and cauliflower in the coconut milk, cover, and let simmer for about 10 minutes.
5. Add chicken and almond butter, cover again, and let simmer for another 6-8 minutes or until chicken is cooked through.
6. Stir occasionally. Add more coconut milk if desired.
7. Consume. BE CAREFUL. Someone I know, who I was cooking for, burnt their mouth badly because they have no patience. And they are very child like. It may or may not have been me....
8. Enjoy!

What changes did you make?

_____

_____

_____

REAL IMPORTANT STUFF...
Kind of:

- *If you add some chicken breasts, broth, and salt and pepper to a crockpot overnight, you'll wake up to shredded chicken that you can add to this dish! Just making your life easier!*
- *Want to make this dish more colorful for guests? Try using purple cauliflower. I don't know why it's purple, but it's exciting. Colors are exciting.*

Bacon Chicken Alfredo

PREP TIME: 20 MINUTES • COOK TIME: 15 MINUTES

SERVES: 2-3

INGREDIENTS

- 1 spaghetti squash, cut in half
- 1 large delicata squash, cut in half
- 1/2 pound chicken tenders
- 4-6 slices bacon, diced
- 1/2 cup canned coconut milk
- 1 teaspoon dried basil
- 1 teaspoon dried parsley
- 1/2 teaspoon garlic powder
- 1/2 teaspoon dried oregano
- 1/4 teaspoon dried thyme
- salt and pepper, to taste

1. Preheat oven to 425°F.
2. Cut spaghetti squash and delicata squash in half and use a spoon to scoop out the seeds and excess threads. Don't be dainty.
3. Place both squashes open-side down on a baking sheet and cook for 20-25 minutes. You will know when they are done cooking when you can poke the outside skin and it 'gives' a bit.
4. Place chicken on a separate foil-lined baking sheet, sprinkle some olive oil (or other kind of fat), over the chicken, salt and pepper it, and sprinkle just a bit of basil on top. Easy peasy. Place in oven and cook for 15-20 minutes.
5. Once the squash is done cooking, pull it out of the oven, and de-thread the spaghetti squash into a large bowl with a fork.
6. Throw the diced bacon into a skillet and cook until done. Use a slotted spoon to pull out the cooked bacon. Pour out half of the bacon fat into a jar and leave half in the skillet.
7. Take the delicata squash and hollow it out with a spoon. Dump the insides of the squash into the warm skillet filled with bacon grease. Then add the coconut milk. You may need to add a little bit more coconut milk, depending on how runny you like your sauce. Mix thoroughly with a ladle to break up the squash a bit.
8. Add seasonings to the mix and salt and pepper as needed. Mix thoroughly and cook on low for about 5 minutes to simmer.
9. Dice up the cooked chicken and add it to the sauce, along with the spaghetti squash threads. Mix well.
10. Top with bacon. Duh. Eat it like you mean it.

What changes did you make?

_____

_____

_____

REAL IMPORTANT STUFF... *Kind of.*

- *Can't find a delicata squash? Try using an acorn squash instead!*
- *Keep your bacon fat! Bacon fat in a jar is a great go-to fat for adding flavor to dishes while you're cooking them.*

Mushroom Chicken

PREP TIME: 10 MINUTES • COOK TIME: 10 MINUTES
SERVES: 4

INGREDIENTS

- 1 pound chicken thighs (I used 4 chicken thighs)
- 1 (14 ounce) can coconut milk
- 3 tablespoons freshly grated ginger
- 1 package shitake mushrooms, sliced
- 1 package crimini mushrooms, sliced
- 2 garlic cloves, minced
- 1/2 sweet onion, thinly chopped
- 1 teaspoon garlic powder
- 1 teaspoon onion powder
- salt and pepper, to taste
- 1-2 tablespoons fat of choice (I used coconut oil)

1. Let's get you prepared. Preparation is key. You will need two separate skillets for this meal. One large, one medium.

2. Place the large skillet over medium heat and add a bit of fat along with the minced garlic and onion. Cook until onions are translucent.

3. Add the can of coconut milk and mushrooms, letting them cook down. Reduce the heat and let those flavors simmer. Reducing the heat is important so the coconut milk doesn't play splishy splash on your counters/stove top... like it did on mine.

4. Once the mushrooms become tender, use your zester to add fresh ginger directly into the pan. Mix together. Add salt and pepper to taste and cover to simmer while you cook the chicken next.

5. Put the medium skillet over medium-high heat and add a bit of fat to the pan. While the pan heats up, season the chicken thighs with salt and pepper along with the garlic and onion powder.

6. Add chicken thighs to the pan and cook on both sides for 6-8 minutes, depending on how thick the thighs are.

7. Once the chicken is almost done cooking, add it directly to the coconut milk pan, cover and let cook for about 3-5 minutes to let the chicken absorb some of the liquid.

8. Now they are ready to eat!

What changes did you make?

_____

_____

_____

REAL IMPORTANT STUFF... *Kind of:*

- *Fresh ginger is pretty important here, but if you don't have that on hand, dried ground ginger will work!*
- *This dish would taste awesome on top of a yam or sweet potato. I just know it!*

AVOCADO CILANTRO
Chicken Salad

PREP TIME: 10 MINUTES • COOK TIME: 10 MINUTES
SERVES: 4

INGREDIENTS

- 1 pound chicken, diced and cooked
- 2 avocados, pitted
- 1 bundle cilantro, stems removed
- 3-4 long carrots, shredded
- 3-4 stems celery, diced
- 1 cucumber, diced
- 1 handful sliced almonds
- juice of 1 lemon
- juice of 1/2 lime
- 1/8 teaspoon garlic powder
- salt and pepper, to taste

1. Start by cooking the chicken however you'd like. If you want a more "grilly" flavor, grill it. Or you could boil it. Or cook it on the stovetop or in the oven. After the chicken has cooked, dice it all up.
2. While the chicken cooks, make the dressing. Pull out your wonderful food processor and add avocados, cilantro, lemon, lime, garlic powder, and salt and pepper to the food processor.
3. Mix thoroughly until the avocado becomes a paste. This will take about 1-2 minutes.
4. Once the avocado creamy sauce is beginning to taste delish, add it to the cooked and diced chicken.
5. If you haven't already shredded the carrots or diced the other veggies, do that. I use the shredding attachment on my food processor to shred my carrots.
6. Mix veggies into the chicken salad and add a handful of sliced almonds.
7. Top with salt and pepper and a little leftover cilantro for extra flavor.

What changes did you make?

_____

_____

_____

REAL IMPORTANT STUFF... *Kind of.*

- *Who needs mayonnaise when you have nature's natural mayonnaise (avocados!) at your fingertips? A wise person once told me that. Meaning the Internet.*
- *Add your own spin on this dish. Make a curry chicken salad. Or add poppy seeds and grapes for a Sonoma-like chicken salad!*

INGREDIENTS

- 1 pound chicken, diced
- 1 teaspoon garlic powder
- 1 teaspoon onion powder
- 1 garlic clove, minced
- salt and pepper, to taste
- 2 tablespoons fat of choice (I used coconut oil)

For the cauliflower rice:
- 1 large cauliflower, stem removed, roughly chopped
- 2 plantains, peeled and diced (get the brown ones)
- 1/2 cup cilantro, roughly chopped
- 1/2 cup vegetable broth
- 1 garlic clove, minced
- 1 teaspoon garlic powder

- 1 teaspoon onion powder
- salt and pepper, to taste

For the avocado sauce:
- 2 avocados
- 3 tablespoons olive oil
- 2 tablespoons water
- 1/4 cup cilantro, roughly chopped
- juice of 1 lemon
- juice of 1/2 lime
- juice of 1/2 orange
- 1/2teaspoon garlic powder
- salt and pepper, to taste

Chicken with Cilantro and Plantain Rice

PREP TIME: 15 MINUTES • COOK TIME: 15 MINUTES
SERVES: 3-4

1. Let's get the rice going. Place the chopped cauliflower into a food processor with the shredding attachment and rice all of the cauliflower.

2. Plop 2 tablespoons of fat into a medium saucepan over medium heat and add the minced garlic. Once the garlic becomes fragrant, add the cauliflower rice. Mix around to help coat in the fat. Let cook for about 5 minutes.

3. While the cauliflower rice is cooking, add a medium-large skillet over medium heat and add 2 more plops of fat into the skillet. Then toss in the diced plantains. The plantains will take about 7-9 minutes to cook on all sides, so continuously toss them to keep them from burning and sprinkle in just a pinch of salt. Once the plantains are cooked, place on a paper towel-covered plate to soak up excess fat.

4. Once the rice has begun to cook down, add the vegetable broth, 1 teaspoons garlic and onion powders, and a bit of salt and pepper. Mix, reduce heat and cover to let cook down.

5. While the rice finishes cooking, place the large skillet back over medium heat and add 2 tablespoons of fat, along with a minced garlic clove to the pan.

6. Once the garlic becomes fragrant, add the chopped chicken to the pan, being sure not to overcrowd it. You want the chicken to get a nice crust on the outside. Sprinkle with the rest of the garlic and onion powder and a bit of salt and pepper.

7. After about 2-3 minutes, flip the chicken to cook on the other sides, only moving around the chicken a little bit to keep that crust going.

8. While the chicken finishes cooking, mix 1/2 cup of chopped cilantro into the cauliflower rice, along with the diced plantains and a bit more salt and pepper.

9. Make the avocado sauce by adding all ingredients to a food processor and pureeing until smooth (about 2-3 minutes).

10. Serve chicken along with rice and top off with the avocado sauce. Love life. Smile. Plantains are amazing.

{ *What changes did you make?*

_____

_____

_____

REAL IMPORTANT STUFF... *Kind of:*

- *Plantains are by far my most favorite thing in the entire world. Don't question me. I'm serious.*
- *No food processor? Just make your avocado ingredients like guacamole. Genius!*

Creamy Cajun Chicken Pasta

PREP TIME: 30 MINUTES • COOK TIME: 10 MINUTES

SERVES: 2-3

INGREDIENTS

- 3 hot chicken sausages
- 2-3 tablespoons coconut oil
- 2 garlic cloves, minced
- 1 medium spaghetti squash, cut in half lengthwise, seeds removed
- 1 yellow onion, diced
- 1 tablespoon Cajun seasoning
- 1 (14 ounce) can coconut milk
- 2-3 tablespoons chopped sun-dried tomatoes (in oil or water)
- salt and pepper, to taste
- chopped green onions, to garnish

1. Cook the chicken sausages and spaghetti squash. Preheat oven to 375°F . Place spaghetti squash halves open-side down on a baking sheet and place the chicken sausage in a small baking dish. Put both in the oven to bake for 25-30 minutes, or until spaghetti squash is soft when you press on the outside of the skin. The chicken sausages should be cooked through after about 15-18 minutes, so you may be able to pull those out earlier.

2. Once the sausages are done cooking, let them cool, then chop them into half-inch or 1-inch pieces.

3. When the spaghetti squash is done cooking, use a fork to pull the threads away from   the squash.

4. Place a large skillet over medium heat and add the coconut oil and minced garlic.

5. Once the garlic has become fragrant, add the diced onions and mix until they become translucent.

6. Add the coconut milk directly to the pan as well as the seasonings.

7. Once coconut milk mixture takes on a reddish color, add spaghetti squash, chopped sundried tomatoes, and diced sausages, as well as a bit more salt and pepper.

8. Let simmer for about 5 minutes under low heat.

9. Add to a bowl, garnish with green onions, and eat it up like it's pasta. Faking our taste buds is so fun!

What changes did you make?

_____

_____

_____

REAL IMPORTANT STUFF... *Kind of:*

- *No chicken sausages to be found? Any sausage would work. Or even just plain old diced chicken would be tasty!*
- *Serve this with a refreshing, pallet-cleansing salad. It will balance this dish nicely.*

Southwest Turkey Sliders
OVER AVOCADO SLAW

PREP TIME: 10 MINUTES • COOK TIME: 10 MINUTES

SERVES: 4

INGREDIENTS

For the sliders:
- 1 pound ground turkey
- 1/4 red onion, minced
- 1/4 red onion, thinly sliced
- 1/2 poblano pepper, diced
- 1/2 red bell pepper, diced
- 1 teaspoon ground cumin
- 1/2 teaspoon ground red pepper
- salt and pepper, to taste
- 1 tablespoon fat (I used bacon fat)

For the slaw:
- 1 small head of cabbage or bag of cabbage, chopped
- 2 avocados
- 1 tablespoon olive oil
- 1 teaspoon lime juice
- 1/2 teaspoon lemon juice
- 1 teaspoon ground cumin
- 1/2 teaspoon crushed red pepper
- salt and pepper, to taste

1. First, make the burgers:
2. Add all ingredients for the burgers in a large bowl. Mix well.
3. Shape small burger patties.
4. Heat up a large skillet over medium heat with a bit of fat in it (I used bacon fat) and add sliders. Flip after about 3-5 minutes or when the sides of the sliders begin to turn a white color (meaning they are cooking through).
5. Now, make your slaw:
6. Pull out your handy-dandy food processor, add all your ingredients for the slaw except the cabbage and pulse until smooth.
7. Pour avocado "mayo" on the cabbage and mix. Top off with a bit of salt and pepper.
8. Place cabbage on a plate and top off with sliders!
9. Consume!

What changes did you make?

_____

_____

_____

REAL IMPORTANT STUFF...
Kind of:

- *Ground beef would be a delicious substitute!*
- *Want even more crunch and nutrients in your slaw? Try broccoli slaw!*

31

- 1 pound ground turkey
- 2 large sweet potatoes or yams
- 1/4 cup hot sauce (sugar free)
- 1 tablespoon fat (I used duck fat)
- 1 yellow onion, diced
- 1 garlic clove, minced
- 2 teaspoons chipotle chili powder

- 1 teaspoon ground red pepper
- 1 teaspoon garlic powder
- 1 teaspoon onion powder
- 1/2 teaspoon paprika
- salt and pepper, to taste

Turkey Stuffed Twice Baked Sweet Potatoes

PREP TIME: 15 MINUTES • COOK TIME: 15 MINUTES
SERVES: 3-4

1. Preheat oven to 425°F.

2. Cut sweet potatoes or yams in half, lengthwise and put them face down on a cookie sheet. Put in the oven to cook for about 25-30 minutes, depending how thick they are. You will know when they are done when the skin gives easily when you push on it. If you pull them out early and the inside doesn't come out easily with a spoon, you'll need to cook them a bit longer.

3. While the sweet potatoes cook, put a skillet over medium-high heat. Add a bit of fat to the hot pan, then add the garlic and onions to start cooking down.

4. Once the onions are translucent, add the ground turkey and use a large spoon to break it up to help cook it a bit quicker.

5. When the turkey is half way done cooking, add the spices. Then let the turkey cook completely (until it's no longer pink), and take off heat.

6. Pull the sweet potatoes out of the oven and use a large spoon to scoop out the insides. Be careful to not go totally to the skin or it may tear and you won't be able to use it to hold the meat in. You want the sweet potato skin to act as a shell.

7. Put the insides of the sweet potatoes directly into the turkey pan and mix thoroughly to combine.

8. Scoop out the new mixture and put into the sweet potato skins. You can go as high as you want. Think of it as a loaded baked potato...load it up!

9. Put those loaded sweet potatoes back on the cookie sheet, face up, and back into the oven and cook for 3-5 more minutes just to meld the flavors together and harden the top a bit.

10. Eat them. They are DAMN GOOD. I mean it. Like seriously. Really good.

What changes did you make?

_____

_____

_____

REAL IMPORTANT STUFF... *Kind of:*

- No ground turkey on hand? Try using ground beef or Italian sausage instead!
- Remember when choosing your yams or sweet potatoes to choose the ones that are fat and round. They are easier to stuff, and since you are baking them twice, the skin is less likely to tear!

Beef

I don't know who decided it, but meat on a stick is more fun. Just a fact. Any chance we get to eat with our hands instead of utensils makes us humans happy. Socially acceptable messy eating is the best. That's why people love baby back ribs. Your face and hands become disgusting, but it's somehow considered funny and a good time. Social rules are weird.

One time, my friend Dom and I took on Ethiopian food. I had absolutely no idea what Ethiopian food was like. Literally had no clue what I was walking into. So when my meal was served with no utensils, I felt awkward. I mean, most of the time my hands are covered in chalk from the gym, not exactly suitable for picking up cooked meats with. But I did it anyway. I scooped with my hands. I scooped with the sponge-like bread that was paired with the lamb and beef. And I shoveled that Ethiopian food into my face. Did you know your hands are perfect shovels? Genius.

Has anyone else noticed how manly my hands look? You know what they say, the camera adds ten pounds... to your hands. Yeah, that's what they say. Damn good shovels those hands are. I was created to be around food.

Menu

Time to eat your beef:

MEXICAN-INSPIRED BURGERS

ROASTED GRAPE BACON-WRAPPED FILET
MIGNON

SAGE BISON BURGERS WITH BALSAMIC BACON
APPLE CHUTNEY

PLANTAIN AND MANGO BEEF

SWEET POTATO ENCHILADAS

COFFEE-MARINATED STEAK FAJITAS

SMOKY BACON CHILI

BUTTERNUT SQUASH CURRY CHILI

SAVORY SWEET POTATO MEATLOAF

SPICY MEXICAN STUFFED POBLANOS

CURRY MEATBALLS

TRUFFLE BACON-WRAPPED FILET MIGNON

INGREDIENTS

For the Mexi burgers:
- 1 pound ground bison (or ground beef)
- 1 (6 ounce) can of green chiles
- 1/2 teaspoon paprika
- 1/2 teaspoon salt
- 1/2 teaspoon black pepper
- 1/2 teaspoon chipotle red pepper (or chili powder)

For the toppings:
- 1 (8 ounce) package of mushrooms
- 1 red onion, thinly sliced
- 1/2 14-ounce jar of roasted peppers, sliced
- 2-3 tablespoons coconut oil

- 1/4 teaspoon chipotle red pepper or chili powder
- 1/2 teaspoon red pepper flakes
- salt and pepper, to taste
- 1-2 tablespoons coconut oil

For the Avocado Roasted Red Pepper sauce:
- 2 avocados
- 1/2 14-ounce jar of roasted peppers, sliced
- 1 teaspoon garlic powder
- 1 teaspoon onion powder
- 1/2 teaspoon black pepper
- 1/4 teaspoon salt
- juice of 1/2 lemon

Mexican-Inspired Burgers

PREP TIME: 15 MINUTES • COOK TIME: 15 MINUTES

SERVES: 4

1. Stop being frightened by the ingredient list. It's not that intense. Grow a pair.

2. Okay, so grab a saucepan or skillet and add a bit of coconut oil to it, along with the sliced onions. Let those guys caramelize, stirring them randomly so they don't burn.

3. Grab another skillet, add the coconut oil, mushrooms, roasted peppers and spices and let those cook down for a while.

4. Make the burger patties. Grab a large bowl, add the meat, spices, and green chiles to it and mix thoroughly. Once the burgers are formed, add them to a large greased skillet. If you don't want to skillet them, cook them on the grill, duh. I cover them with a lid to help them cook a bit quicker. Cook for about 5-6 minutes per side, depending how thick they are.

5. While the burgers are cooking, make the avocado sauce. It's insanity. Pull out your food processor, add all ingredients for the sauce to it and puree until smooth. This sauce is almost like a cheese sauce. But without the bloat and gas. How great is that?

6. Once the toppings are cooked, the burgers are cooked to perfection, and the sauce is silky smooth, stack it all up. Burger, sauce, toppings, then some sliced avocado on top. Oh goodness, wow.

What changes did you make?

_____

_____

_____

REAL IMPORTANT STUFF... *Kind of:*

- *This roasted red pepper sauce could be put onto anything. It's like crack... in a good way. Don't be mad I said that.*
- *This meal is the closest I've come to making a guy fall in love with me. It obviously didn't work, but maybe it will work for you. Good luck!*

ROASTED GRAPE, BACON-WRAPPED
Filet Mignon

PREP TIME: 10 MINUTES • COOK TIME: 25 MINUTES

SERVES: 2

INGREDIENTS

- 1 1/2 cups red grapes
- 2 filet mignons
- 2 strips of bacon
- 2 tablespoons balsamic vinegar
- 1 tablespoon coconut oil
- pinch of salt

1. Preheat oven to 400°F.
2. Place a piece of parchment paper in an 8x12 glass baking dish (for easy clean up, but no big deal if you don't have any).
3. Combine grapes with balsamic vinegar and coconut oil in baking dish. Top with a bit of salt and toss to coat.
4. Roast grapes for about 25 minutes in the oven or until soft.
5. When there is about 10 minutes left for the grapes to cook, pull out a medium skillet and place over medium heat.
6. While the skillet heats up, wrap the bacon around the outer rim of the filet mignon. Use a toothpick to press through part of the meat to connect the bacon ends. Don't let that bacon sneak away from your meat!
7. Salt both sides of the filet mignon, just a little bit.
8. Cook bacon on all sides for about a minute each side, then place the filet mignon into the bacon fat that has seeped onto the pan and cook for around 5-6 minutes per side (this time will depend on how thick your filet mignon is and how you prefer yours. I prefer medium rare).
9. Top filet mignon with roasted grapes and a bit of the leftover balsamic vinegar that is reserved in the baking dish.
10. Be incredibly happy.

What changes did you make?

_____

_____

_____

REAL IMPORTANT STUFF... *Kind of:*

- *If you add some chicken breasts, broth, and salt and pepper to a crockpot overnight, you'll wake up to shredded chicken that you can add to this dish! Just making your life easier!*
- *Want to make this dish more colorful for guests? Try using purple cauliflower. I don't know why it's purple, but it's exciting. Colors are exciting.*

38

Sage Bison Burgers
WITH BALSAMIC BACON APPLE CHUTNEY

INGREDIENTS

PREP TIME: 20 MINUTES • COOK TIME: 15 MINUTES

SERVES: 2-3

For the burgers:
- 1 pound ground bison
- 2 tablespoon fresh sage, chopped
- 1 teaspoon garlic powder
- 1 teaspoon onion powder
- salt and pepper, to taste
- 1-2 tablespoons choice of fat (I used bacon fat)

For the chutney:
- 5-6 slices bacon, diced
- 1 red onion, diced
- 1 apple, cored and diced
- 2 tablespoons balsamic vinegar
- 2 tablespoons water
- pinch of salt

1. Place large skillet over medium heat and add diced bacon. Cook down until bacon is completely cooked through, then place cooked bacon on a plate with a paper towel. Leave 2-3 tablespoons of bacon fat in the pan.
2. Add the diced onion to the hot pan and cook down until translucent.
3. Add the apple and mix with onion and cover to let cook for 4-5 minutes.
4. Add the balsamic vinegar, water and a bit of salt and thoroughly mix together until the balsamic vinegar is completely combined, then add the bacon back in and reduce heat.
5. While the chutney is keeping warm, mix all of the burger ingredients together in a bowl.
6. Make 4 burger patties and place burgers in a skillet over medium heat with 1-2 tablespoons of your choice of fat. Bacon fat is a good choice.
7. Cook on both sides for about 5-8 minutes or until cooked to preference.
8. Place chutney on top of burgers and consume!!

{ *What changes did you make?*

_____

_____

_____

REAL IMPORTANT STUFF...
Kind of:

- *No ground bison? It's cool, ground beef works just great!*
- *Stop worrying about what kind of apples will taste best in this meal. They're covered in bacon fat. They'll taste good no matter what. Trust me.*

INGREDIENTS

For the marinade:
- 1 1/2 cups brewed coffee
- 1 tablespoon coconut aminos
- 1 tablespoon white wine vinegar
- 1 teaspoon chili powder
- 1 teaspoon salt

For the rub:
- 2 tablespoons ground coffee
- 1/2 teaspoon cinnamon
- 1/2 teaspoon cumin
- 1/2 teaspoon smoked paprika
- salt and pepper, to taste

For the fajitas:
- 1 pound sirloin steak
- 1 red onion, sliced
- 1 poblano pepper, sliced thin
- 1 yellow bell pepper, sliced thin
- 1 orange bell pepper, sliced thin
- 2 tablespoons fat (I used bacon fat)
- juice of 2 limes
- juice of 1/2 lemon

Coffee-Marinated Steak Fajitas

PREP TIME: 24 HOURS • COOK TIME: 25 MINUTES
SERVES: 2-4

1. You should marinate the steak overnight. If you can't do that, at least marinate for a couple hours. Just throw all the marinating ingredients into a big plastic bag or container, along with the sirloin steak, and throw it in the fridge to marinate all night long. A plastic bag full of happiness.

2. Once the steak is done marinating, place the rub seasonings on a plate, pull the steak out of the marinade, and cover the steak on both sides with the rub.

3. Heat up a skillet with 1 tablespoon of fat, and when the skillet is super hot, add the sirloin steak to it. Mine was pretty thick, so I cooked it on both sides for about 5-7 minutes. You only want to flip the steak once, because you don't want to overcook it! So don't touch it a ton.

4. While the steak is cooking, heat up another skillet with another tablespoon of fat and add the onions, poblano pepper, and bell peppers.

5. Let the veggies cook down, stirring randomly to make sure they do not burn.

6. Once the sirloin steak is done cooking, pull it off the stovetop and let sit for about 5 minutes. There are a ton of juices in there, and you don't want them to leak out! Let the meat rest!!

7. When the meat has rested, thinly slice the steak and throw it in the pan with the fully cooked veggies. Squeeze the lime and lemon on top! You just want to incorporate some of the steak juices and flavors, so it shouldn't be for more than 20 seconds. If it's longer, the meat may get tough.

8. Salt and pepper the fajitas and serve with a side of guacamole or sliced avocado!

What changes did you make?

_____

_____

_____

REAL IMPORTANT STUFF... *Kind of:*

- *Coconut aminos taste similar to soy sauce and can often be found at natural food stores. It's awesome. Can't find it at your store? Order online. Hello!! The internet is a wonderful thing.*
- *Use your favorite peppers in your fajitas. Make it taste exactly how you want it to!*

Plantain and Mango Beef

PREP TIME: 10 MINUTES • COOK TIME: 10 MINUTES

SERVES: 1-2

- 1 (12 ounce) sirloin steak, sliced into 1/4-1/2 inch pieces
- 1 yellow onion, sliced
- 2 garlic cloves, minced
- 1 plantain, ends removed, peeled and sliced into 1/4 inch pieces, smashed with the bottom of a drinking glass (use a slightly ripe plantain that is brown-spotted in color)
- 1 mango, peeled and cubed
- 2 teaspoons curry powder
- 1 teaspoon garlic powder
- 1 teaspoon red pepper
- salt and pepper, to taste
- 2 tablespoons fat of choice (I used coconut oil)

1. Heat a large skillet over medium heat and add a tablespoon of coconut oil, then add 2 minced garlic cloves and sliced onions.

2. While the onions begin to cook down, place a medium saucepan over heat and add two tablespoons of coconut oil. When the oil is hot, add the smashed plantains and let cook for about 3-5 minutes per side, careful not to burn them (like I'm good at).

3. While the plantains cook, add the sliced sirloin steak to the onion pan. Use tongs to flip the meat continuously so it doesn't overcook.

4. Once the meat has almost cooked through (2-3 minutes), add the mango, garlic powder, red pepper, salt and pepper and mix thoroughly.

5. Cook for another 1-2 minutes until meat is cooked to your preference and spices are thoroughly incorporated, then remove from heat.

6. When the plantains are cooked (they'll look brown) on both sides, remove from heat, place on a paper towel to remove the excess oil, then add to the beef and mango mixture.

7. Consume!

What changes did you make?

_____

_____

_____

REAL IMPORTANT STUFF... *Kind of.*

- *These plantains can be slippery, so be careful when smashing them. A mallet would work, but I don't have one of those on hand.*
- *If I drank red wine, or knew anything about wine at all, I'm betting it would pair great with this dish. Just sayin'.*

Curry Meatballs

PREP TIME: 8 MINUTES • COOK TIME: 10 MINUTES
SERVES: 3-4

For the balls:
- 1 pound ground beef
- 1/2 yellow onion, diced
- 2/3 cup almond flour
- 2 eggs
- 2 teaspoons curry powder
- 2 teaspoons garam masala
- 1/2 teaspoon ginger
- just a hint of cinnamon
- salt and pepper to taste
- 1-2 tablespoons coconut oil for cooking

For the saucy flare:
- 1 1/2 to 2 cups canned coconut milk (the more the better)
- 1 cup organic chicken broth
- 1/2 yellow onion, diced
- 5 teaspoons curry powder
- 2 teaspoons garam masala
- 1 teaspoon ginger

1. Add all ingredients for the meatballs to a large bowl and thoroughly mix together.
2. Shape meatballs to the size you like. Mini meatballs or large ones are both acceptable!
3. In a large skillet or pot, add the coconut oil, then add the meatballs and diced onions from the sauce ingredients and let them brown for a couple minutes. Let the meatballs cook on both sides for about 3-4 minutes.
4. Once the onions and meatballs have browned a bit, add the rest of the ingredients for the sauce and mix together until meatballs are covered in sauce.
5. Cover and let meatballs and sauce simmer until it thickens and meatballs have cooked through, about 5 minutes.

What changes did you make?

_____

_____

_____

REAL IMPORTANT STUFF... *Kind of:*

- For a leaner meat, you could easily use ground chicken or turkey for this recipe.
- If you're not a huge fan of curry, tone down the amount you add in so your pallet isn't freaked out. I love curry so I think the more, the better!

43

INGREDIENTS

For the enchiladas:
- 3 sweet potatoes or yams
- 1 pound grass-fed ground beef
- 1/2 yellow onion, diced
- 2 garlic cloves, minced
- (4 ounce) can diced green chiles
- 1/2 teaspoon cumin
- 1/4 chili powder
- 1/4 sea salt
- 1/4 black pepper
- 3-4 tablespoons coconut oil

For the sauce:
- 1 (14 ounce) can tomato sauce
- 1/4 yellow onion, minced
- 1/3 cup vegetable broth
- 1 tablespoon coconut oil
- 1/2 teaspoon garlic powder
- 1/2 teaspoon oregano
- 1/2 teaspoon chili powder
- salt and black pepper, to taste

Sweet Potato Enchiladas

PREP TIME: 25 MINUTES • COOK TIME: 15 MINUTES

SERVES: 4

1. Preheat oven to 350°F.

2. Make "tortillas" from the sweet potatoes, using a mandolin to slice the sweet potatoes lengthwise (you can use a knife, but I found I couldn't get the same thinness using a knife).

3. Heat up a large skillet and place 2 tablespoons of coconut oil in it. When skillet is very hot and coconut oil has melted, add the sweet potatoes. Cook the sliced sweet potatoes for 3-5 minutes per side or until sweet potatoes are soft. You DO NOT want them crispy. Do as many batches as you need to and place sweet potato slices on a paper towel to remove excess oil and cool while you cook the meat.

4. While the sweet potatoes are cooling, use the same skillet to cook the meat. Add in a bit of oil, then add the minced garlic cloves along with the onion.

5. When the onions become translucent, add in the ground beef, along with the green chiles and spices. Let that cook down until it is cooked through completely, using a wooden spoon to break up the ground beef and mix thoroughly.

6. While the meat cooks, place a saucepan over medium heat for the sauce. Add a tablespoon of oil along with the minced onion.

7. When the onion becomes translucent, add the tomato sauce and vegetable broth, as well as all the seasonings. Reduce heat and let that cook down until it thickens just a bit.

8. Once everything is done cooking, it's time to use your fingers!

9. Pull out an 8x8 or 9x9 glass baking dish, add a spoonful of enchilada sauce on the bottom and start building the enchiladas.

10. Each enchilada should take 3 slices of a sweet potato. Place the slices down on your cutting board, overlapping them each slice onto the one before it. Now place a spoonful or two of the meat mixture in the center of the sweet potatoes, then wrap the sweet potatoes over the meat, tucking the ends in (like a tortilla).

11. Repeat until all the sweet potatoes are gone. If you have leftover meat, place that around the enchiladas.

12. Pour the enchilada sauce on top.

13. Place in oven and bake for 15 minutes.

14. Let cool, then eat your heart out!

What changes did you make?

_____

_____

_____

REAL IMPORTANT STUFF... *Kind of:*

- *Some of my readers had a hard time making the sweet potatoes into tortilla shapes. Their easy fix for this issue: sweet potato enchilada lasagna. My blog readers are awesome.*

Smoky Bacon Chili

PREP TIME: 10 MINUTES • COOK TIME: 20 MINUTES

SERVES: 2

- 1 pound ground beef
- 6 slices of bacon, cubed
- 1 yellow onion, diced
- 1 red pepper, diced
- 1 green pepper, diced
- 1 garlic clove, minced
- 1 (14 ounce) can of fire roasted tomatoes
- 1 (8 ounce) can of tomato sauce
- 1 tablespoon garlic powder
- 1 tablespoon chili powder
- 2 tablespoons smoked paprika
- 2 teaspoons cumin
- 1 teaspoon cayenne pepper
- salt and pepper, to taste
- 2-3 sweet potatoes or yams (optional

1. Preheat oven to 400°F. Poke holes in the sweet potatoes with a fork. Place on rack in oven and cook for about 30-40 minutes or until potato is soft and cooked through.
2. Pull out a large pot, add the cubed bacon and let cook down.
3. While the bacon is cooking, chop all the veggies.
4. When the bacon has browned and is a bit crisp, add the veggies.
5. Let cook for about 6 minutes or so, then add the ground beef and all the spices.
6. Once the beef is browned, add the tomato sauce and fire roasted tomatoes.
7. Mix well and let all the flavors meld together while cooking on low for the next 8 minutes or so, stirring occasionally.
8. Split open the sweet potato, pour the chili over it, and eat. Delicious!

What changes did you make?

_____

_____

_____

REAL IMPORTANT STUFF...
Kind of:

- If you want to cook your sweet potato quicker, cut it in half lengthwise and bake for half the time!
- Adding a lil' extra crispy bacon on top would be make this chili even more perfect. More is always better when it comes to bacon.

Butternut Squash Curry Chili

PREP TIME: 15 MINUTES • COOK TIME: 25 MINUTES

SERVES: 4-5

- 1 1/2 pounds ground beef
- 1/2 pound ground pork
- 1 large butternut squash, peeled and cubed
- 1 red bell pepper, diced
- 1 green bell pepper, diced
- 1 yellow bell pepper, diced
- 1 yellow onion, diced
- 6 garlic cloves, minced
- 1 (14 ounce) can tomatoes, diced
- 1 (14 ounce) can tomato sauce
- 1 cup chicken or beef stock
- 1/2 cup canned coconut milk
- 3 tablespoons coconut butter
- 1 tablespoon fat of choice (I used coconut oil)

Spice mixture:
- 3 tablespoons curry powder
- 2 tablespoons chili powder
- 2 tablespoons cumin
- 1 tablespoon paprika
- 2 teaspoons garlic powder
- 2 teaspoons salt
- 2 teaspoons cinnamon
- 2 teaspoons cocoa powder
- 2 teaspoons garam masala
- 1 teaspoon ground cloves
- salt and pepper, to taste

1. Heat up a large pot over medium-high heat with a tablespoon of some kind of fat. Add the beef and ground pork and let it brown. Cook for about 5-8 minutes.
2. While the meat is cooking, chop all the veggies and squash.
3. Once meat is cooked, remove with a slotted spoon and set aside in a bowl.
4. Add the minced garlic cloves to the same pot and once they become fragrant, add the diced veggies and cook for about 5 minutes.
5. Add the chicken stock, tomato sauce, diced tomatoes, and coconut milk to the pot. Mix together. Cover and cook until butternut squash is tender. About 10-15 minutes.
6. Add spices and beef/pork back to the pot. Stir to combine. Last, add coconut butter and mix thoroughly.
7. Decrease heat and let simmer for about 5 minutes to let all the flavors combine.
8. Consume. Be careful. The squash will hold a hell of a lot of heat.

What changes did you make?

_____

_____

_____

_____

REAL IMPORTANT STUFF...
Kind of:

- *A slice of avocado on top is a perfect garnish since it's a natural cooling agent. I don't know if that's true, but that's what my taste buds say.*

Savory Sweet Potato Meatloaf

PREP TIME: 10 MINUTES • COOK TIME: 45 MINUTES

SERVES: 4-5

- 2 1/2 pounds ground beef
- 1 sweet potato or yam, shredded
- 1 sweet yellow onion, finely chopped
- 1 pound uncured bacon, diced
- 1 cup almond flour/meal
- 2 eggs
- 1/4 cup raisins
- 1/4 cup golden raisins
- 1/2 tablespoon cinnamon
- 1 teaspoon garlic powder
- 1 teaspoon onion powder
- salt and pepper, to taste

1. Preheat oven to 400°F.
2. Time to get the meatloaf 'insides' ingredients going. So take 1/2 pound of the bacon and chop it up into bite-size pieces. Add to a deep skillet and begin to cook down. Once the fat has begun to render, add the chopped onions and raisins to the pan to cook with the bacon.
3. While those ingredients cook together, shred the sweet potato either in your food processor with the shredding attachment or with a cheese grater. Whatever you have on hand!
4. Once the bacon is cooked through, the onions are slightly translucent, and the raisins have begun to bloat (you'll see what I mean) add them to a large bowl along with all other ingredients: beef, sweet potatoes, almond meal, eggs, and all seasonings.
5. Use your hands and get dirty. Mix all ingredients thoroughly together and press meat into 2-3 bread loaf pans, depending on their size. I sometimes use the disposable ones, because then there is no clean up. I'm dirty enough as it is.
6. Top off the meatloaf with the extra slices of bacon.
7. Bake for 40-45 minutes.

What changes did you make?

_____

_____

_____

REAL IMPORTANT STUFF... *Kind of:*

- The picture may not show it, but this is honestly one of my favorite dishes. All the sweet and salty flavors pair perfectly with each other. Trust me. Try it.
- This is even awesome as leftovers. So even if it makes more than you can handle in one meal, you'll have many more the rest of the week!

48

SPICY MEXICAN-STUFFED
Poblanos

PREP TIME: 15 MINUTES • COOK TIME: 25 MINUTES
SERVES: 3-6

INGREDIENTS

- 6 poblano peppers, tops cut off and seeds removed
- 1 pound ground beef
- 1/2 yellow onion, diced
- 3 garlic cloves, minced
- 1 (6 ounce) can tomato paste
- 1 (6 ounce) can diced green chiles
- 2 tablespoons hot sauce
- 1/2 tablespoon garlic powder
- 1/4 teaspoon ground red pepper
- 1/8 teaspoon paprika
- salt and pepper, to taste
- 1-2 tablespoons fat of choice (I used bacon fat)

1. Preheat oven to 350°F.
2. Heat up a large skillet with some fat over medium-high heat.
3. Add the garlic and cook until it becomes fragrant, then add the diced onions. Let the onions cook down until they become translucent.
4. Add the ground beef to cook down.
5. Once the ground beef is turning brown, add the rest of the ingredients, except for the poblano peppers.
6. While the flavors meld, cut the tops off of the poblanos and rinse them inside and out to get rid of the extra seeds. Cut a slit down the side of them and stuff them with the cooked meat.
7. Place them on a baking sheet lined with parchment paper or foil and bake for 20-25 minutes or until the poblanos begin to blister and soften.
8. Eat them. I let mine sit for a bit. Actually I let them sit overnight since I cooked them at 11:30 at night. Probably should eat them while they are still warm. Just sayin'.

What changes did you make?

_____

_____

_____

REAL IMPORTANT STUFF...
Kind of:

- *Can't find any poblano peppers? Any other kind would work! Choose your favorite or try just stuffing bell peppers.*
- *This is one of those meals that is amazing because your food is held in a pocket. So it's pretty much like eating a sandwich. But not really.*

INGREDIENTS

- 1 spaghetti squash, cut in half lengthwise, excess seeds removed
- 1 (8 ounce) package of baby Portobello mushrooms, sliced
- 1/2 yellow onion, thinly sliced
- 3 tablespoons truffle oil
- 2 filet mignons
- 2 pieces of bacon
- 2 garlic cloves, minced
- 1 teaspoon garlic powder
- salt and pepper, to taste

Truffle Bacon-Wrapped Filet Mignon

PREP TIME: 30 MINUTES • COOK TIME: 15 MINUTES

SERVES: 2

1. Preheat oven to 400°F.

2. Place spaghetti squash halves open-side down on a baking sheet. Bake for 25-30 minutes or until squash is soft when you press on the outside of the squash. Do not overcook.

3. Once the squash has cooled for a couple minutes, use a fork to pull the threads from the squash. Like spaghetti. Get the name now? Good.

4. When the spaghetti squash is cooling, pull out two medium skillets and place one over medium heat.

5. Add a tablespoon of truffle oil to the hot pan as well as the minced garlic cloves. Add the sliced mushrooms and diced yellow onion to the fragrant garlic pan and mix around to coat in the truffle oil.

6. Let the mushrooms and yellow onions cook down until the onions become translucent, and then add the garlic powder and a bit of salt and pepper.

7. Heat the second skillet over medium heat. Wrap the bacon around the outer rim of the filet mignon. Use a toothpick to press through part of the meat to connect the bacon ends.

8. Salt both sides of the filet mignon, just a little bit.

9. In a very hot skillet, place the bacon sides onto the hot skillet to release some of the fat to cook the meat on. Cook bacon on all sides for about a minute each side.

10. Place the filet mignon into the bacon fat and cook for around 4-5 minutes per side. (Time will depend on how thick your filet mignon is and how you prefer yours cooked. Mine was cooked to medium rare).

11. While the filet mignon finishes cooking, mix the spaghetti squash threads into the mushroom and onion pan and finish off with two more tablespoons of truffle oil and some salt and pepper. Mix thoroughly.

12. Once the filet mignons are done cooking on both sides, add spaghetti squash mixture to a plate, top with filet mignon, and a bit of dried basil on top for a bit more flavor. Love the amazing flavor of truffle oil in all of its glory.

What changes did you make?

_____

_____

_____

REAL IMPORTANT STUFF...
Kind of.

- I can hear you now. "Truffle oil is expensive, Juli. You must be high." And I know it's a pretty penny. BUT a little goes a LONG way. You'll have truffle oil in your cabinet for a long time, so your money will go far. Believe me, it took me about a year to finally buy it. But it's TOTALLY worth it!

Pork

Even though my cookbook shows me spending time with only one woman (her name is Laura), I actually do spend time with the opposite sex. Mostly in the gym, in the form of a guy friend, but at least it's a start.

I have this issue with dating, and I proclaim that problem often on my blog. I guess I really want to make it clear to the World Wide Web that dating is the bane of my existence. You know, because everyone totally cares.

So thank gosh I finally have another outlet to proclaim my dating frustrations on. A cookbook, the perfect place! Dating has truly become this unknown, foreign thing to me. I always had boyfriends growing up, always had crushes. But it turns out, when you get older and don't have hormones pumping through you like a fire hose (weird analogy), you don't have constant crushes on people. AND you tend to have higher expectations of the opposite sex.

The more I go on dates, the more I don't want to go on dates. Having to ask people questions, having to waste money on someone you probably won't ever see again, and having to force a smile that looks incredibly awkward is NOT what I call an exciting Friday night.

Now what I do think is a fantastic weekend is watching Sex and the City reruns with Laura, in my pajamas, with no makeup on, while consuming far too many paleo treats that I bake up.

After writing that last sentence, I think I'm pretty cool with staying single for a good twenty more years.

Menu

Pork is totally better than chicken.
Totally.

BLACKBERRY-GLAZED GRILLED PORK CHOPS

AVOCADO CHORIZO SWEET POTATO SKINS

APPLE AND BACON ROSEMARY PORK BURGERS

SAUSAGE SPAGHETTI SQUASH BAKE

PEACH AND BASIL GRILLED PORK CHOPS

PORK SATAY

STUFFED SWEET PORK LOIN

INGREDIENTS

- 1-2 pounds pork chops (bone-in or boneless, either will do!)
- 1 teaspoon cinnamon
- 1/2 teaspoon dried thyme
- salt and pepper, to taste
- 12 ounces fresh blackberries
- 1/2 cup balsamic vinegar
- 2 tablespoons water
- pinch of salt

Blackberry-Glazed Pork Chops

PREP TIME: 10 MINUTES • COOK TIME: 15 MINUTES
SERVES: 2-4

1. Turn your grill on to a medium-high heat!! If you don't know how to light it, I can't help you.
2. Place pork chops on a plate and cover them in cinnamon, thyme, salt and pepper on both sides. Press seasonings into pork chops.
3. While your grill heats up, place a small saucepan over medium heat on your stove top and add blackberries, balsamic vinegar, water, and a pinch of salt.
4. Let the sauce begin to break down, stirring frequently to make sure it doesn't burn on the bottom.
5. Turn heat to low and let the sauce simmer for about 3-5 minutes.
6. Pour half of the sauce into a bowl (you can leave the blackberries in the saucepan because you'll just use them to top your chops off later).
7. Use a glazing brush to glaze one side of the pork chop then place that glazed side down onto your grill.
8. Glaze the other side, cover grill and let cook for 5-7 minutes per side, depending on the thickness of your chop. I glazed each side of my pork chop probably 3-4 times to make sure as much blackberry sauce as possible could be soaked up by the chop. Make sure your chop is cooked on both sides and cook completely through before removing from grill. (Took me about 12-14 minutes total).
9. Once the pork chops are all done cooking, add to plate and top with the leftover blackberry sauce that has been simmering and thickening up.
10. Eat until you cry. So delicious.

What changes did you make?

_____

_____

_____

REAL IMPORTANT STUFF... *Kind of:*

- *No grill? That's okay! Just cook your pork chops on the stove top, making sure your skillet is nice and hot!*
- *No blackberries in season where you are? Frozen will do. OR you can even use blueberries for this recipe.*

AVOCADO CHORIZO
Sweet Potato Skins

PREP TIME: 15 MINUTES • COOK TIME: 25 MINUTES
SERVES: 3-6

INGREDIENTS

- 1 pound chorizo (no sugar added)
- 3 sweet potatoes or yams (long, skinny ones work the best for this)
- 1/2 red onion, diced
- 2 ripe avocados, halved and pits removed
- juice of 1/2 lime
- juice of 1/2 lemon
- 1 teaspoon cumin
- 2 tablespoons coconut oil, melted
- salt and pepper, to taste
- 1 tablespoon almond flour

1. Preheat oven to 425°F.
2. Use a fork to poke some holes in the sweet potatoes. Place on a baking sheet and bake for 35-40 minutes or until sweet potatoes are soft when you poke them.
3. While the sweet potatoes are baking, pull out a large skillet, place over medium heat and add the chorizo to it. Use a wooden spoon to break up the chorizo while it cooks.
4. When the chorizo is halfway done cooking, add the onions to sweat them out.
5. When the chorizo is cooked completely through, put the chorizo mixture on a plate with a paper towel to soak up some of the excess fat, and let cool.
6. Pull out your handy dandy food processor. Use a spoon to scoop out the inside of the two avocados and place in the food processor. Mix until you get a smooth paste.
7. Add lime, lemon, cumin and a bit of salt. Pulse until mixed thoroughly.
8. Place the chorizo and 3/4 of the avocado mixture in a large bowl to incorporate. Leave the other 1/4 of avocado mixture for toppings.
9. When the sweet potatoes are done cooking, let cool, cut in half, scoop out insides (leaving about 1/2-1 inch of sweet potato still inside) of sweet potato, and use a pastry brush to brush coconut oil on the inside and all around the sweet potato shell.
10. Place back on baking sheet and in the oven for another 10-15 minutes or until crispy.
11. Once sweet potatoes are crispy, put the avocado and chorizo mixture into the sweet potato, top off with a little sprinkle of almond flour, and place back in the oven for around 5 minutes.
12. Top off the sweet potato skins with some leftover avocado mixture (similar to a scoop of sour cream on top). Diggin' it.
13. Finally consume!

What changes did you make?

_____

_____

_____

REAL IMPORTANT STUFF...
Kind of.

- *Need to cook these quicker? Try cutting them in half, lengthwise, and cooking them in half the time!*
- *Can't find any sugar-free chorizo? Just add minced garlic cloves, chili powder, dried oregano, cumin, cinnamon, and salt and pepper to your ground pork to get a similar flavor.*

Spaghetti Squash Bake

PREP TIME: 25 MINUTES • COOK TIME: 20 MINUTES

SERVES: 3-4

INGREDIENTS

- 1 pound bulk mild pork Italian sausage
- 1 medium spaghetti squash, cut in half, lengthwise, and seeds removed
- 1 bundle of kale, roughly chopped
- 1 red onion, halved and sliced
- 1 egg
- 1/3 cup chicken broth
- 1/2 cup canned coconut milk
- 1 garlic clove, minced
- 1 tablespoon garlic powder
- 1 teaspoon tarragon
- 1 teaspoon salt
- 1/2 teaspoon black pepper
- 1/4 teaspoon ground sage

1. Preheat oven to 400°F.
2. Place spaghetti squash halves open-side down on a baking sheet and bake for about 20-25 minutes or until you can press into the squash and it gives a bit. Be sure not to overcook, it becomes very mushy!
3. While the squash bakes, heat up a large pot over medium-high heat and add the Italian sausage. Break up with a wooden spoon or spatula.
4. Once the sausage is cooked through, remove with a slotted spoon and put in a bowl.
5. Keep the extra fat from the meat in the pot, add the minced garlic and add the kale, onions, and chicken broth. Combine.
6. Add the coconut milk and spices. Cover and let simmer for about 5 minutes.
7. Pull the spaghetti squash out of the oven and de-thread with a fork.
8. Once the kale is wilted and the onions become translucent, remove from heat and add the spaghetti squash as well as the egg to the kale/onion mixture. Mix thoroughly.
9. Then add the cooked Italian sausage and mix together.
10. Place the mixed ingredients into a 9x12 glass baking dish and spread out evenly.
11. Bake 15-20 minutes or until top is slightly browned.
12. Consume!

What changes did you make?

_____

_____

_____

REAL IMPORTANT STUFF...
Kind of:

- *Are pork sausages on sale at your market? Perfect. Just remove the casing and use the insides as bulk sausage. Save your pennies wherever you can.*
- *No kale? It's cool. Spinach it up.*

- 1 to 1 1/2 pounds ground pork
- 6-8 strips of bacon, cut into 1 inch pieces
- 1 apple, cored and diced
- 1-2 tablespoons rosemary (dried or fresh)
- salt and pepper, to taste

Apple and Bacon Rosemary Pork Burgers

PREP TIME: 10 MINUTES • COOK TIME: 15 MINUTES

SERVES: 3

1. Heat-up a medium-sized skillet over medium heat.
2. Chop up the bacon and add it to the pan.
3. Let bacon cook for a bit until some of the fat seeps out and the ends of the bacon begin to turn up.
4. Then add the apple to begin to cook down. Bacon fat was going bat sh*t crazy, so I covered it with a lid.
5. While the bacon and apple are cooking for the next 5-7 minutes, throw the ground pork in a bowl, add the rosemary and salt and pepper and use your hands to combine everything! If you don't use your hands, it won't taste right. Just trust me. Buck-up child.
6. Once the bacon and apples are done cooking, use a slotted spoon to remove and add them to a paper towel on a plate to let cool. Leave behind 2-3 tablespoons of bacon fat in the pan.
7. Time to make the patties!! Take a small ball of meat, I'd say smaller than a lacrosse ball, ball it up and then smash it down with your thumbs to make a damn good looking patty. You want this a bit thinner than a normal burger.
8. Make another!
9. Place a spoonful of the bacon and apple mixture on top of one of the patties, then plop another patty on top, then use your fingers to seal up the sides. A pinching technique works best. Pinch a ton to make sure the burgers stay shut while they cook.
10. Repeat. I got 3 burgers out of 1 pound of ground pork.
11. Reheat the skillet with the leftover bacon fat in it.
12. Add the stuffed burgers to the pan. Cook for about 5-7 minutes per side (depending on the thickness).
13. Eat them on up!!

{

What changes did you make?

_____

_____

_____

REAL IMPORTANT STUFF... *Kind of:*

- *Too lazy to make stuffed burgers? That's cool, I get it. Just make your burgers separate from the apple and bacon and top your burgers off with the mixture. Same thing, different outfit.*

Pork Satay

PREP TIME: 15 MINUTES • COOK TIME: 10 MINUTES

SERVES: 4

- 1 pound boneless pork tenderloin
- 1 small onion, finely diced
- 1/4 cup almond butter (or sunflower seed butter)
- 3-4 tablespoons coconut aminos
- 2 tablespoons raw honey
- 1/4 cup water
- 3 tablespoons coconut oil
- 2 garlic cloves, minced
- 1/4 teaspoon ground ginger
- sprinkle of red pepper flakes
- salt and pepper, to taste

1. Light that grill of yours to medium-high heat!
2. In a small saucepan, add 2 tablespoons of coconut oil. Add garlic cloves and onions and begin to cook down.
3. When the onions have become translucent, add almond butter, 1 tablespoon coconut oil, coconut aminos, honey, water, ginger, red pepper flakes, and a bit of salt and pepper into your saucepan and mix well.
4. Let simmer, uncovered for 6-8 minutes.
5. Once sauce has thickened, reserve about 1/3-1/2 cup of the sauce.
6. It's time to make the pork skewers. Cut the pork loin in half widthwise then cut each half into thin strips.
7. Thread the pork onto soaked wooden or metal skewers.
8. Use a glazing brush to brush some of the sauce onto the pork skewers, then place the skewers onto a grill, uncovered. Cook for about 3-4 minutes per side, or until there is no longer any pink remaining on the meat.
9. Pour extra sauce over the skewers and serve. Delish!

What changes did you make?

_____

_____

_____

REAL
IMPORTANT
STUFF...
Kind of.

- No grill? How about this... dice up your pork tenderloin, cook it on the stovetop in a pan with some coconut oil, then pour your sauce on top. Pure genius, that's what I am.
- Need a perfect side dish for this meal? Cauliflower rice would be wonderful. Especially my coconut cauliflower rice. Legit.

Peach and Basil Pork Chops

PREP TIME: 1 HOUR • COOK TIME: 15 MINUTES
SERVES: 4

INGREDIENTS

- 4 boneless pork chops
- 2 peaches, cut in half, pits removed
- Fresh basil leaves, stems removed
- 3 tablespoons olive oil
- 1-2 tablespoons white wine vinegar
- 2 teaspoons dried thyme
- salt and pepper, to taste

1. Marinate the pork chops for at least an hour! Place the pork chops into a plastic bag and then add olive oil, white wine vinegar, dried thyme and a bit of salt and pepper, and place in the fridge to keep fresh.
2. Once the pork chops have marinated, remove them from the fridge to come to room temperature. And then heat up your grill to medium-high!
3. Cut the peaches in half, remove pits, and rub a bit of olive oil and white wine vinegar on the insides of the peaches. You won't need much.
4. Place pork chops on grill along with the peaches. Place peaches on the upper part of the grill so they don't char.
5. Cook pork chops on both sides for about 5-7 minutes or until completely cooked through, depending on their thickness.
6. Cook peaches for 3-4 minutes per side.
7. When the pork chops are done cooking, move to a plate and place a peach half on top.
8. Use a knife to cut 3 slits in the peaches.
9. Add fresh basil, folding the leaves in half and pressing them into the peach slits.
10. Eat up!!

What changes did you make?

_____

_____

_____

REAL IMPORTANT STUFF... *Kind of.*

- No grill? Cook your pork chops on the stovetop or bake in the oven!
- If you can't grill your peaches, you could dice them up and roughly chop your basil to make a delicious chutney to top your pork chops with!

61

INGREDIENTS

- 1 1/2 to 2 pounds boneless pork tenderloin
- 1/2 sweet potato or yam, diced
- 1 yellow onion (1/2 diced, 1/2 sliced-for topping)
- 1/2 apple, diced
- 1/2 cup raisins
- 1/3 cup walnuts, chopped
- 2 tablespoons fresh sage, chopped
- 2 garlic cloves, minced
- 2 tablespoons coconut oil
- 1 tablespoon apple cider vinegar
- 1 lemon, sliced
- juice of 1 lemon
- 2 tablespoons balsamic vinegar
- salt and pepper, to taste
- butcher's twine, cut into 5-6 inch pieces, for wrapping the pork tenderloin

Stuffed Sweet Pork Loin

PREP TIME: 10 MINUTES • COOK TIME: 25-30 MINUTES

SERVES: 4

1. Preheat oven to 375°F.
2. Place a large skillet over medium heat and add 2 tablespoons of coconut oil to the pan. Then toss in garlic cloves, diced apples, diced onions, and diced sweet potatoes. Cover to let steam for about 5 minutes to help cook through, stirring often to keep from burning.
3. It's time to prepare the pork loin for the stuffing. This is probably the most complicated part of it all, but don't worry, if you mess up you can just fix it with butcher's twine.
4. I imagine my pork loin like a pumpkin roll, and I want to unroll that pumpkin roll. So place the tenderloin on a cutting board, then holding your knife parallel to your cutting board, cut 1/2" above the underside of the roast and begin slicing inward, down the entire roast, while unrolling the meat (imagine that you're trying to slice through the cream cheese of a pumpkin roll… you with me here?). Continue slicing inward and down the roast until it is an open blanket of meat on your board.
5. You can either use a mallet to pound the meat thinner or leave as is. I left mine as is, but pounding it down will make it easier to roll. I like making my life harder. I'm hardcore like that.
6. Once the sweet potatoes have become soft in the pan, add in chopped walnuts, raisins, sage, and then add in the apple cider vinegar and a bit of salt and pepper.
7. Place the butcher's twine on your cutting board, spacing each piece out 1 inch from the next, then place the pork loin on top.
8. Spread the sweet potato ingredients throughout the pork loin, making sure to keep level throughout.
9. Roll the pork loin tightly, and then begin tying the twine. I like to tie off the ends first to make sure nothing can seep out. Tie all twine pieces tightly and cut off excess twine.
10. You'll want to sear the pork. Heat up the large skillet again and add a bit of extra fat to the pan. When the pan is very hot, add the pork loin to sear on all sides for 2-3 minutes.
11. Once the pork loin has seared, place it in a 9x13 glass baking dish and lay out the extra sliced onions and lemons throughout and on top of the pork loin.
12. Pour a bit of balsamic vinegar on the top of the pork loin, along with some salt and pepper.
13. Place in the oven and cook for 30-35 minutes. Then let the pork rest for about 5 minutes before slicing into the meat and eating that all up!

What changes did you make?

_____

_____

_____

REAL
IMPORTANT
STUFF…
Kind of.

- *This dish could use some green! Serve your sliced pork loin with some kale sautéed in minced garlic. Perfect meal!*

Fish / Seafood

I honestly hate cooking with fish or any sort of seafood. Not sure why, but I highly dislike it. If it weren't for having a blog, I literally would never cook with it. I feel very much like a fish out of water with seafood. Bad analogy. How's this one... I feel like a cat in water. Picture it, do it. Not so pretty. This fact is probably because I live in a landlocked state and have no fresh seafood at my fingertips. That's an excuse. Either way, I don't like cooking with fish. But it's delicious and lovely, so I'm forced to.

When I started writing my blog, I honestly had no idea how to cook. I had just graduated from college and was living with my parents. So most of the meals that I made for myself came from a box that I heated up in the microwave. So when I decided to try eating paleo and writing a blog about it, I kind of needed to figure out what the hell I was doing. I started off by spending hours upon end searching for delicious paleo recipes and trying to understand what the hell sautéing and braising meant.

I never really figured out those two things. But I did find out that I REALLY liked to cook, even if I didn't know what I was doing. Cooking became this calming habit. It felt like I was finally in control of what I was putting into my body. And I finally didn't feel sick anymore, as I had my whole life. The coolest part was I was actually having fun cooking; it wasn't a chore. I began trying new foods I would have never touched the year before and actually enjoyed eating them. My poor mother had 18 difficult years of my stubborn eating, and now I was finally eating anything I found at the store. That sweet woman. If we only had known about paleo eighteen years earlier and if I had not known about oatmeal cream pies, life would have been so much simpler for her.

Menu

Seafood is scary, so let's make it easy:

GRILLED SWORDFISH WITH PEACH AND AVOCADO SALSA

THAI COCONUT LIME SHRIMP

CITRUS MANGO SPICY TILAPIA AND KALE

OPEN-FACE SHRIMP BURGERS OVER CHARRED PLANTAINS

RED CURRY SCALLOP SOUP

PINEAPPLE SHRIMP CEVICHE

Grilled Swordfish
WITH PEACH AND AVOCADO SALSA

INGREDIENTS

PREP TIME: 1+ HOUR • COOK TIME: 10 MINUTES

SERVES: 2

For the swordfish marinade:
- 2 swordfish filets
- 1 tablespoon coconut oil
- 1 tablespoon apple cider vinegar
- 1 teaspoon honey
- juice of 1 lemon
- 1 garlic clove, minced
- pinch of cayenne pepper
- pinch of salt and pepper

For the salsa:
- 2 peaches, seed removed, diced
- 1 avocado, halved and diced
- 1 garlic clove, minced
- 1/4 red onion, finely chopped
- 1/2 jalapeño, finely chopped
- handful of cilantro, roughly chopped
- juice of 1 lime
- salt, to taste

1. Place the marinade ingredients in a shallow bowl and mix together. Then put the swordfish in the marinade and flip on both sides to coat. Leave in fridge for 1+ hours.
2. Make the salsa. Mix all salsa ingredients together in a large bowl. Place in fridge to chill.
3. Once the swordfish has marinated, light your grill and bring to medium heat.
4. When your grill is nice and hot, place the swordfish on the grill and cook for about 3-5 minutes on each side.
5. Top the swordfish off with the salsa and love life. OMG good.

What changes did you make?

_____

_____

_____

REAL IMPORTANT STUFF...
Kind of:

- *No swordfish around? You could use some gorgeous ahi tuna steaks instead!*
- *The first time I had swordfish was in high school at the restaurant I worked in. It was way more elegant than my swordfish. Way more expensive too. Mine's better though. Just a fact.*

Thai Lime Coconut Shrimp

PREP TIME: 10 MINUTES • COOK TIME: 10 MINUTES

SERVES: 2-4

- 1 pound raw shrimp, peeled and deveined
- 1 (6 ounce) can coconut milk
- 3 egg whites, whisked
- 1/3 cup coconut flour
- 1 cup unsweetened shredded coconut
- 3 tablespoons curry powder
- 1 teaspoon cayenne pepper
- 1/2 teaspoon Sriracha
- 1/2 teaspoon sea salt
- 1/2 teaspoon black pepper
- 1 garlic clove, minced
- 1 tablespoon fat (I used coconut oil)
- juice of 1 lime

1. Grab 3 bowls. Stop complaining. In the first bowl, whisk the egg whites until they are foamy. In the second bowl, mix the coconut flour with 2 tablespoons curry powder, cayenne, salt and pepper. Then add the shredded coconut to the third bowl.

2. Let's get the shrimp ready. Lay out all 3 bowls along with a plate to place them on when coated. First, dip the shrimp in the egg, lightly coat with the coconut flour, then finish off coating with the shredded coconut.

3. Once all the shrimp are covered in happiness, heat up a large skillet. Add your fat of choice along with the minced garlic clove.

4. Once the garlic becomes fragrant, add coconut milk, Sriracha, and 1 tablespoon of curry powder. Mix together and let it cook down for about 1 minute over medium heat. Once it is bubbly and starting to thicken, add the shrimp. Let cook on both sides for about 2-3 minutes or until they are pink and the tails begin to curl in.

5. When they are about done, squeeze the lime all over.

6. Serve. Honestly, they rock even more the next day. With avocado. Oh sh*t yeah!

What changes did you make?

_____

_____

_____

REAL IMPORTANT STUFF... *Kind of:*

- These would be great party appetizers. Just push them onto skewers and let your guests enjoy.
- Serve this alongside wilted greens sprinkled with salt and lime to make your meal complete!

- 5-6 tilapia filets
- 1 tablespoon cayenne pepper
- 1 teaspoon smoked paprika
- 1/2 teaspoon red pepper flakes
- 1-2 bundles of kale, chopped or torn apart
- 1 mango, thinly sliced
- 3-4 garlic cloves, minced
- 4-6 tablespoons fat of choice (I used coconut oil)
- 2 oranges, halved
- 2 limes, halved
- 2 lemons, halved
- salt and pepper, to taste

Citrus Mango Spicy Tilapia and Kale

PREP TIME: 10 MINUTES • COOK TIME: 15 MINUTES
SERVES: 4-6

1. Let's get to it! Pull out a large skillet and a medium skillet. If you have two large ones, that would work even better! Also pull out a shallow bowl or plate to hold the spices.

2. Heat up 2-3 tablespoons of coconut oil over medium-high heat in a large pan. While the pan heats, add spices to the bowl, along with some salt and pepper, and lay the fish in the bowl to completely cover both sides in the spices.

3. Add fish to the hot, greased pan and let cook on both sides for about 3-4 minutes. When you flip the fish to cook on the second side, squeeze half a lemon, lime and orange directly on top of the fish and add the sliced mango. Mix around a bit to season the mango with some of the leftover spices.

4. While the fish cooks, add the remaining coconut oil to the second pan and add the minced garlic to cook down a bit. Once the garlic becomes fragrant, add in the chopped kale. Squeeze the other halves of the lemon, lime, and orange on top of the kale and mix around a bit with a large spoon. Once the kale is covered in coconut oil and the citrus juices, add 1 teaspoon of water and cover to help the kale cook down. Keep an eye on it and mix it around a bit if needed; no need to burn it!!

5. Once the kale is sautéed up and the fish is done cooking, add the kale to a plate and top off with a tilapia filet, along with a few slices of mango on top. Bomb.

What changes did you make?

_____

_____

_____

REAL IMPORTANT STUFF... *Kind of:*

- *Sweet mango and spicy fish were made in the world of love. If that doesn't make sense, guess you need to try this recipe.*
- *No kale? No worries. Try spinach or some kind of collard green. It will taste delicious no matter what.*

Red Curry Scallop Soup

PREP TIME: 10 MINUTES • COOK TIME: 10 MINUTES

SERVES: 3-4

INGREDIENTS

- 1 pound scallops (bay or sea scallops will do)
- 1 (14 ounce) can coconut milk
- 2-4 ounces red curry paste
- 1 red bell pepper, sliced
- green onions, chopped (to garnish)
- 2-3 tablespoons fat of choice (I used coconut oil)
- 1 garlic clove, minced
- salt and pepper, to taste

1. Place a large skillet over medium heat and add your fat of choice and garlic clove to the pan.
2. As soon as the garlic becomes fragrant, add scallops to the pan, being sure not to overcrowd the pan so you can get a nice crust on the scallops. Sprinkle with a bit of salt.
3. Cook on both sides for about 2-3 minutes until golden brown. Then place the scallops on a plate while you get the soup ready.
4. In the same hot pan, add the red bell peppers. As soon as the peppers begin to wilt some, add the coconut milk and red curry paste.
5. Mix well to help the curry paste break down, then add the salt and pepper.
6. Once the soup ingredients are mixed well, add the soup to a bowl, then add as many scallops as you would like, and top with green onions.

What changes did you make?

_____

_____

_____

REAL IMPORTANT STUFF... *Kind of:*

- *Want to make this more like a noodle bowl? Add some baked spaghetti squash threads to your bowl and you got yourself an even heartier meal.*
- *I made this meal one time when I was absolutely desperate for food and too incredibly lazy to make it. It's simple and quick so no excuses when it comes to this meal!*

Pineapple Shrimp Ceviche

PREP TIME: 15 MINUTES • FRIDGE TIME: 1+ HOUR

SERVES: 4+

INGREDIENTS

- 1 pound medium-small shrimp, peeled and deveined, cooked, roughly chopped
- 1 cup pineapple, diced
- 1 avocado, diced
- 3-4 stalks of celery, diced
- 1/2 red onion, diced
- 1 serrano chile, seeds removed, minced
- 1 jalapeño pepper, seeds removed, minced
- 1 cup grape tomatoes, halved
- juice of 5 limes
- juice of 5 lemons
- juice of 1 orange
- course sea salt, to taste
- 1 cup cilantro, chopped
- 1 cup avocado, diced

1. Add all ingredients, except for cilantro and avocado, to a large glass bowl.
2. Mix well.
3. Place in the refrigerator for an hour or more.
4. Before serving, add in cilantro and avocado and mix again.
5. Eat up!! Soooo easy!

What changes did you make?

_____

_____

_____

REAL IMPORTANT STUFF... *Kind of:*

- Ceviche is better the longer it sits. So let it sit around for a while in that fridge of yours. You won't be disappointed.
- No shrimp on hand? That's ok. You could make this with tilapia, lobster, or halibut instead!

71

INGREDIENTS	• 1 pound raw, peeled and deveined shrimp
	• 1 cup almond flour
	• 1 egg, lightly beaten
	• 2 tablespoons Dijon mustard
	• juice of 1/2 a lime
	• 1/2 teaspoon onion powder
	• 1/4 teaspoon cayenne pepper
	• 2 garlic cloves, minced
	• salt and pepper, to taste
	• 1 yellow onion, thinly sliced
	• 2-4 tablespoons fat of choice (I used coconut oil)
	• 1 avocado, sliced to garnish
	• 2 plantains, peeled and cut in half lengthwise

Open-Face Shrimp Burgers
OVER CHARRED PLANTAINS

PREP TIME: 10 MINUTES • COOK TIME: 15 MINUTES
SERVES: 4-6

1. Place shrimp in your food processor and pulse until chopped.

2. Pour the shrimp into a bowl and add egg, almond flour, mustard, lime, onion powder, cayenne pepper, salt and pepper, then mix until combined.

3. With the mixture, form patties to your preference, being sure to squeeze them tightly to help keep them from breaking apart.

4. Place a large skillet over medium heat and add a bit of fat to the pan. Cook patties until gorgeously golden on both sides. Mine took about 4-5 minutes per side to completely cook through. While the burgers cook, put another skillet over medium heat and add a bit of fat.

5. Place the halved plantains into the hot pan and sprinkle with salt. Cook on both sides for 5-6 minutes, getting a nice char on the outside. Then set aside.

6. In that same skillet that you just cooked the plantains, add a bit of fat and toss in the sliced onions with a bit of salt to begin to caramelize.

7. Once the onions are cooked to your preference, place charred plantains on a plate, top with the shrimp burger, the onions and a bit of avocado.

8. Enjoy the simple pleasure of a no bun lifestyle.

What changes did you make?

_____

_____

_____

REAL IMPORTANT STUFF... *Kind of:*

- *I love plantains. Like, OMG-love them. So they create the perfect bedding for these shrimps burgers. When you want bread, eat plantains. Works every time. Kind of.*
- *No shrimp? Another hardy fish will do just fine for burgers! Lobster burgers... ummmm, YUM!*

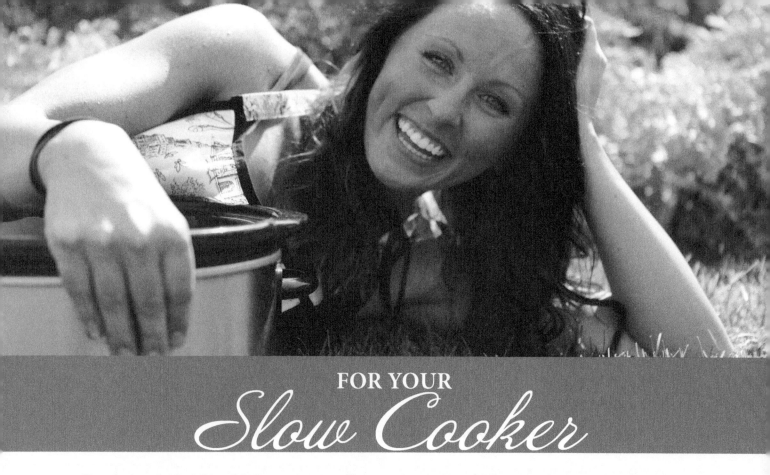

FOR YOUR
Slow Cooker

If you're uncomfortable with these pictures of me cuddling my slow cooker in a flower garden, you're dull. Sorry my relationships are different. I don't discriminate. And honestly, my slow cooker seems to always appreciate me and never do me wrong. I have yet to have a bad meal come out of my slow cooker. So, we have formed a very close bond.

If you don't have a slow cooker yet, you NEED to buy one. RIGHT NOW. They are a fool-proof tool that makes eating healthy EXTREMELY easy. Okay, I'll stop with the capital letters. But really, if you are a person who loves to make excuses as to why you can't eat paleo, because it's soooooo time consuming, this will erase that excuse. And you'll have to find something else to complain about. Tough life.

Slow cookers have truly saved my life. Because

I spend most of my time either in a coffee shop on my computer or in the gym, I need food ready to go at all times. It's pretty cool I get to do what I love for a living: food and exercise. I once was told that I need to get help for my obsessions with food and exercise. But I see those kinds of obsessions as blessings. I spend my days trying to become healthier and stronger than I was the day before. That does not make me psychotic. That does not make me crazy. I am already those two things without exercise and food. But to make that person happy, I will admit the following:

My name is Juli and I am obsessed with exercise, food, and my slow cooker. I am admitting my problems now so I can work on my habits. By that I mean cooking more food in the crockpot on a weekly basis and spending even more time squatting in the gym. Squatting is the best.

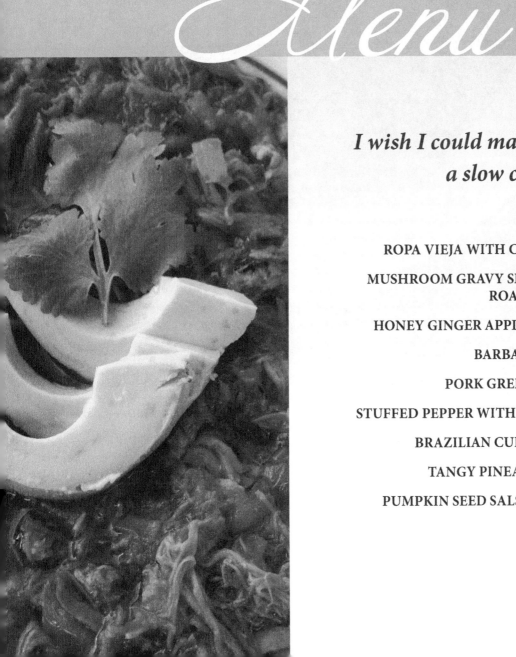

Menu

I wish I could make everything in a slow cooker:

ROPA VIEJA WITH CUBAN STYLE RICE

MUSHROOM GRAVY SLOW-COOKED RUMP
ROAST

HONEY GINGER APPLE SHREDDED PORK

BARBACOA

PORK GREEN CHILE

STUFFED PEPPER WITH SPANISH STICKY RICE

BRAZILIAN CURRY CHICKEN

TANGY PINEAPPLE PORK

PUMPKIN SEED SALSA CHICKEN STEW

For the ropa vieja:
- 1 1/2 to 2 pounds beef chuck roast, trimmed of extra fat
- 1 yellow onion, thinly sliced
- 1 red bell pepper, thinly sliced
- 1 yellow bell pepper, thinly sliced
- 1 (6 ounce) can tomato sauce
- 1 (14 ounce) can diced tomatoes
- 3 tablespoons capers, drained
- 1 tablespoon cumin
- 1 tablespoon dried thyme
- 1 tablespoon dried oregano
- 4 garlic cloves, peeled
- 1 bay leaf
- salt and pepper, to taste

For the Cuban rice:
- 1 head of cauliflower, stem removed and roughly chopped
- 3 thick slices of bacon, diced
- 1 (4 ounce) can tomato sauce
- 2 teaspoons cumin
- 1 teaspoon garlic powder
- 1 teaspoon onion powder
- salt and pepper, to taste

Ropa Vieja with Cuban Style Rice

PREP TIME: 20 MINUTES • COOK TIME: 6-8 HOURS
SERVES: 4-6

1. Pull out your handy dandy slow cooker.

2. Add onions and peppers to the bottom of it.

3. Plop the chuck roast on top, cut 4 deep slices into the chuck roast and push the garlic cloves into the roast.

4. Add all the spices and salt and pepper. Then add the tomato sauce, diced tomatoes, capers, and bay leaf to the rest of the slow cooker.

5. Cook on low for 6-8 hours or high for 5-7 hours.

6. When the ropa vieja is almost done, it's time to cook the rice.

7. Add the chopped cauliflower to a food processor with the shredding attachment, and rice all the cauliflower.

8. Add the diced bacon to a large saucepan and cook until bacon is browned and cooked almost completely through.

9. Add the cauliflower, tomato sauce and spices to the saucepan. Mix thoroughly, then cover.

10. Let cook for about 10-12 minutes, stirring randomly to help incorporate all the flavors.

11. Once the ropa vieja is done cooking, use a couple forks to shred the beef in the crockpot. Serve ropa vieja on top of the sautéed cauliflower rice

12. Consume. A lot. And love every second of it.

What changes did you make?

_____

_____

_____

REAL IMPORTANT STUFF... *Kind of:*

- *No food processor? That sucks. Buy one. Best investment ever. Or use a cheese grater to grate your cauliflower. That can just get REAL messy.*

MUSHROOM GRAVY
Slow-Cooked Rump Roast

INGREDIENTS

PREP TIME: 10 MINUTES • COOK TIME: 6-8 HOURS

SERVES: 4-6

- 1-2 pounds beef rump roast
- 3-4 cups chicken broth (no sugar added)
- 2 large onions, roughly chopped
- 5-6 garlic cloves, peeled
- 1 (8 ounce) container of mushrooms, sliced
- salt and pepper to taste
- 1 teaspoon garlic powder
- 1 teaspoon onion powder
- 1/2 teaspoon paprika
- 1/2 cup full-fat coconut milk, canned

1. Pull out that handy slow cooker of yours!
2. Add in the broth, coconut milk, onions, garlic, mushrooms, and spice to your slow cooker and mix together.
3. Make a little room in your slow cooker around the mushroom mix and plop that cute little rump roast in the pot.
4. Turn on low for 6-8 hours.
5. Then you eat it!! Holy moly, THAT WAS EASY!!

What changes did you make?

_____

_____

_____

REAL IMPORTANT STUFF...
Kind of.

- *The more mushrooms you add, the better. Those things seem to disappear in the slow cooker. MORE MUSHROOMS!*
- *Roasted broccoli tastes great with this meal. For reals. I've tried it*

78

HONEY GINGER APPLE
Shredded Pork

PREP TIME: 10 MINUTES • COOK TIME: 6-8 HOURS

SERVES: 4-6

INGREDIENTS

- 2 pound boneless pork shoulder roast (or any other roast you prefer)
- 1 yellow onion, sliced
- 2 apples, cored and sliced
- 2/3 cup beef or chicken broth OR water
- 1 tablespoon raw honey
- 2 tablespoons freshly grated ginger (use ground ginger if you don't have fresh on hand)
- 1 teaspoon cinnamon
- 1 teaspoon salt
- 1/2 teaspoon smoked paprika
- 1/2 teaspoon pepper
- 2 garlic cloves, peeled and smashed
- 1 bay leaf

1. Pull out your slow cooker.
2. Add broth or water, then onions, then pork, then apples then all spices and bay leaf.
3. Cover.
4. Cook for 8-10 hours on low or 6-8 hours on high.
5. Use tongs or a fork to shred the pork.
6. Consume. Warning: food may be hot. Speaking from experience.

What changes did you make?

_____

_____

_____

REAL IMPORTANT STUFF...
Kind of.

- *Make sure to put your apples on top of the roast so they don't turn to applesauce in the cooking process.*
- *An attractive male on Instagram made his own version with an apple, ginger, cinnamon, and maple-pulled pork. I love him. He's a food genius.*

Barbacoa

PREP TIME: 10 MINUTES • COOK TIME: 6-8 HOURS

SERVES: 4-6

- 1 1/2 to 2 pounds beef rump roast, trimmed of extra fat
- 6-8 garlic cloves, peeled
- 2-4 bay leaves
- 1/4 cup apple cider vinegar
- 1/4 cup vegetable broth
- 1 yellow onion, roughly chopped
- 1/2 red onion, roughly chopped
- 1 tablespoon cumin
- 2 chipotle peppers in adobo sauce, roughly chopped
- 1 tablespoon adobo sauce (from the can of chipotle peppers)
- 1 (8 ounce) container of chopped mushrooms (optional)

- salt and pepper, to taste

For the second round of cooking:
- 1 (16 ounce) can tomato sauce
- 1 (12-16 ounce) can green chiles
- 1 tablespoon chipotle chili powder
- 2 teaspoons cayenne pepper
- 1 teaspoon ground red pepper
- 1/2 teaspoon smoked paprika
- 1/2 teaspoon nutmeg
- 1/4 teaspoon ground cloves
- salt and pepper, to taste

1. Pull out your slow cooker. Actually, just leave it on your counter like me. It gets used a lot. If it doesn't, shame on you!
2. Add to your crock pot: garlic cloves, bay leaves, apple cider vinegar, broth, chopped onions, cumin, chipotle peppers and sauce, mushrooms, salt, pepper, and rump roast. Mix ingredients around to help coat the rump roast.
3. Cover and let cook for 6 hours on high or 8 hours on low. Run a fork along the rump roast at the end of cooking to make sure it is done and easily shreddable (word? I don't think so).
4. Once the roast is done cooking:
5. Use a couple forks to shred the meat in your crockpot.
6. Discard the bay leaves.
7. Add tomato sauce, green chiles, and spices. Mix thoroughly
8. Let cook on high for 30 minutes-1 hour.
9. Eat that b*tch up!

{ *What changes did you make?*

_____

_____

_____

REAL IMPORTANT STUFF... *Kind of:*

- *This recipe was inspired in attempt to recreate my favorite "fast food" meal. I had always loved their barbacoa, but was sick of spending $10 for a tiny meal. This is the perfect, cheap substitute.*
- *Be sure to use all the spices. It will make all the difference.*

Pork Green Chile

PREP TIME: 10 MINUTES • COOK TIME: 6-8 HOURS

SERVES: 4-6

- 2 pound boneless pork shoulder roast
- 1 yellow onion, chopped
- 2 garlic cloves, minced
- 3 (4 ounce) cans diced green chiles
- 2 Anaheim chilis, seeds removed, diced
- 1 poblano pepper, seeds removed, diced
- 1-2 jalapeño peppers, seeds removed, diced

- 2 cups chicken or beef broth (no sugar added)
- 1 (8 ounce) can of diced tomatoes
- 1 teaspoon dried oregano
- 1 teaspoon salt
- 1 teaspoon white pepper
- 1/2 teaspoon cumin
- 1/2 teaspoon dried sage
- 1/2 teaspoon paprika
- 1/2 teaspoon cayenne pepper

1. Pull out your slow cooker.
2. Place the pork roast in the slow cooker and place all the veggies around it.
3. Pour the green chiles and tomatoes over the pork.
4. Toss in all the spices on top.
5. Pour the broth in the slow cooker.
6. Turn the slow cooker on low for 6-8 hours.
7. Once the time has elapsed, use some tongs to shred the pork and mix all the ingredients together.
8. Consume!!

What changes did you make?

_____

_____

_____

REAL IMPORTANT STUFF...
Kind of:

- *Got leftovers? You got a perfect breakfast at your fingertips. Add to eggs and sweet potatoes and make an amazing scramble!*
- *Want to save your eyes from burning when you end up accidentally touching them after cutting the peppers?! Wear gloves. Easy fix. And your eyes will thank you.*

For the peppers:
- 4 bell peppers (whichever color you like best)
- 2 pounds ground beef
- 1/3 head of cauliflower
- 6 ounce can tomato paste
- 1 yellow onion
- 1 garlic cloves, minced
- 1/2 jalapeño, minced
- 1/2-2/3 cup beef broth
- 1 tablespoon garlic powder
- 1 tablespoon onion powder
- 2 teaspoons cumin
- 1 teaspoon tarragon
- 1/2 teaspoon chili powder

For the rice:
- 2/3 head cauliflower
- 1/2 yellow onion, minced
- 2 garlic cloves, minced
- 1 (6 ounce) can tomato paste
- 1/2 jalapeño, minced
- 1/3 cup salsa, your choice (no sugar, please and thank you)
- 1/4 cup beef broth
- 1 tablespoon garlic powder
- 1 tablespoon onion powder
- 2 teaspoons cumin
- 1 teaspoon tarragon
- 1/2 teaspoon chili powder
- 2 tablespoons olive oil

Stuffed Pepper with Spanish Sticky Rice

PREP TIME: 10 MINUTES • COOK TIME: 6-8 HOURS
SERVES: 4-6

1. To make the peppers:
2. Pull out your always-amazing food processor AND slow cooker. My first loves.
3. Cut the stem off the cauliflower and add roughly 1/3 of it to the food processer, using the shredding attachment to rice the cauliflower.
4. Add the cauliflower to a large bowl.
5. Switch the shedding attachment out for the blade and add the roughly chopped onion to the food processer along with the garlic clove and jalapeño.
6. Once the mixture is processed, add it to a large bowl and add the ground beef, tomato paste, and spices. Mix well to combine.
7. Cut the tops off the peppers, pull out the tops along with the seeds, and stuff the meat mixture into them.
8. Place them in the slow cooker and pour the beef stock in the bottom. You will most likely have extra meat leftover, so just stuff that in the crevices around the peppers.
9. To make the sticky rice: (make right before you are ready to eat the peppers)
10. You will need the food processor once again for this one, and a large sauté pan.
11. Add the rest of the cauliflower to your food processor, using the shredding attachment to rice the cauliflower.
12. When the cauliflower is riced, add it to a large pan with 2 tablespoons of fat, along with the minced onion, garlic and jalapeño.
13. Add the tomato paste, salsa, beef broth, and spices and combine.
14. Once it is mixed thoroughly, turn the burner down low and let it simmer for about 5-8 minutes, stirring occasionally to make sure it does not stick to the bottom.
15. When the rice is all cooked through and nice and sticky, plate it with a stuffed pepper on top. EAT IT UP. I love faux rice.

What changes did you make?

_____

_____

_____

REAL IMPORTANT STUFF...
Kind of:

• *No food processor? That sucks. Buy one. Best investment ever. Or use a cheese grater to grate your cauliflower. That can just get REAL messy.*

Brazilian Curry Chicken

PREP TIME: 10 MINUTES • COOK TIME: 6-8 HOURS

SERVES: 4-6

- 1 1/2 to 2 pounds chicken breasts (or whatever suits your fancy)
- 3/4 cup canned coconut milk
- 1 cup chicken broth
- 2 tablespoons tomato paste
- 3 garlic cloves, minced
- 1 tablespoon ground ginger
- 4-6 tablespoons curry powder
- 1 red bell pepper, chopped
- 1 yellow bell pepper, chopped
- 1 yellow onion, thinly sliced
- salt and pepper, to taste
- dash of red pepper flakes

1. Grab your slow cooker!
2. Add in the coconut milk, tomato paste, garlic, ginger, curry powder, salt and pepper, red pepper flakes, and whisk together.
3. Add in peppers and onions.
4. Add in chicken and pour broth over the chicken.
5. Mix all ingredients together to completely cover the chicken in the curry mixture.
6. Cover and cook at low for 6-8 hours or high for 4-5 hours.
7. Then eat it in a cute Tupperware bowl. Or on a plate. Whatever suits your fancy.

What changes did you make?

_____

_____

_____

REAL IMPORTANT STUFF...
Kind of:

- *Someone once told me that Brazilian food and curry do not mix, and shouldn't ever. I obviously did not listen. And am glad I didn't, because this is delicious. Never believe authority. Make your own rules!! Yeah, be careful with that advice.*

Tangy Pineapple Pork

PREP TIME: 10 MINUTES • COOK TIME: 6-8 HOURS
SERVES: 4-6

- 2 pound boneless pork shoulder
- 2 cups pineapple, cubed
- 4 garlic cloves, peeled
- 1 yellow onion, sliced
- 1 red bell pepper, sliced
- 1/2 cup vegetable broth
- juice of 1 lemon
- juice of 2 limes
- zest of 1 lime
- 1 teaspoon cayenne pepper
- salt and pepper, to taste
- diced green onions, to garnish

1. First cut 4 slits in the pork shoulder and press the garlic cloves into those slits. Then place pork shoulder in your slow cooker.
2. Pour in the vegetable broth.
3. Place the onions, bell peppers, and pineapple in the slow cooker around and on top of the pork shoulder.
4. Add the lime and lemon juices on top of the pork.
5. Add the lime zest, cayenne pepper, salt and pepper.
6. Cover and let cook on low for 6-8 hours.
7. Once the pork is done cooking, use tongs to shred the pork, then top with diced green onions.

What changes did you make?

_____

_____

_____

REAL IMPORTANT STUFF... *Kind of:*

- *No pineapple? Mango would be awesome in this recipe!*
- *Want this pork to be a bit more on the spicy side? Try adding some red pepper flakes for a little more kick.*

INGREDIENTS

- 3-4 chicken thighs
- 2 cups chicken broth
- 1 1/2 cups pumpkin seeds (pepitas)
- 1/4 cup olive oil
- 2 tomatoes, roughly chopped
- 1 jalapeño, stem and seeds removed, roughly chopped
- 1 garlic clove, peeled
- 2 tablespoons fresh cilantro
- salt and pepper, to taste
- 1 yellow onion, sliced
- 1 green bell pepper, stem and seeds removed, sliced
- 1 red bell pepper, stem and seeds removed, sliced
- extra cilantro, to garnish
- sliced avocado, to garnish

Pumpkin Seed Salsa Chicken Stew

PREP TIME: 10 MINUTES • COOK TIME: 6-8 HOURS
SERVES: 4-6

1. You need to roast the pumpkin seeds for the pumpkin salsa. Place a small skillet over medium heat and add a tablespoon or so of olive oil along with the pepitas in the pan.
2. Roast for about 3-4 minutes, continuously moving them around in the pan to be sure they do not burn.
3. Once the pepitas are roasted, place in your food processor and puree.
4. Once the pepitas have broken down, add tomatoes, jalapeños, garlic clove, 2 tablespoons of cilantro, salt and pepper. Puree until you get a chunky salsa.
5. Time for your slow cooker. Add the sliced onions to the slow cooker, then place the chicken thighs on top.
6. Salt and pepper the chicken then pour the pumpkin seed salsa on top of the chicken.
7. Top off with the red and green bell peppers. Cover and let cook on low for 6-8 hours.
8. Once the time has elapsed, use tongs to shred up the chicken and create the stew.
9. Pour in a bowl, top with cilantro and avocado and enjoy the slow-cooked flavors!

What changes did you make?

_____

_____

_____

REAL IMPORTANT STUFF... *Kind of:*

- *I got the inspiration for this recipe while sitting on the floor of an airport, waiting for a delayed flight, reading a food magazine. Mexican food is cool. And freaking delicious.*
- *You don't even have to make this as a stew! You could just serve it as chicken thighs. The chicken is tender and super moist. How chicken should ALWAYS be. Moist. What a gross word.*

SWEET & SAVORY
Breakfasts

I love breakfast. I mean LOVE it. Back in the day, when I used to eat the ever-incredibly-delicious-sugar-blasted cereal, I would go to bed dreaming about my breakfast. That's how you know you're a foodie. Or have an addiction. Either way, if you go to bed thinking about your next meal, you're just as weird as I am. You food-obsessed junkie, you.

But when I switched over to the paleo lifestyle, it took me a while to fall in love with breakfast again. To me, meat for breakfast sounded like eating soiled socks. My own soiled socks. And that's bad, trust me. I couldn't fathom cooking up meat and eating it with a side of vegetables. Gag me. So I slowly began to eat some paleo pancakes for breakfast. Then tried out eggs. Then move on to some breakfast sausage. And before I knew it, I was scarfing down leftover fajitas with my morning Americano. Amazing how our taste buds change over time.

But if you're not on the "fajitas for breakfast" train yet, that's okay, I'll convert you over time. In the meantime you can try some of my frittatas, pancakes, and waffles. And fall in love with breakfast all over again. And me. Preferably if you're a male.

Menu

What the hell am I going to eat for breakfast??

BREAKFAST MEATZA

CARAMELIZED ONION FRITTATA

MEXICAN HASH EGG BAKE

GRILLED SALMON AND ASPARAGUS FRITTATA

STUFFED ACORN SQUASH

CARAMELIZED PLANTAIN PANCAKES WITH
SWEET CINNAMON PLANTAIN MAPLE SYRUP

CHERRY JAM CREPE STACK

DOUBLE CHOCOLATE WAFFLES

CHOCOLATE BANANA BREAKFAST BARS

BLUEBERRY WAFFLES WITH BLUEBERRY MAPLE
COMPOTE

Breakfast Meatza

PREP TIME: 10 MINUTES • COOK TIME: 10 MINUTES

SERVES: 4

1. Preheat oven to 350°F.
2. Place the breakfast sausage in a medium bowl and crack an egg directly in. Mix with your hands until the egg is broken up and you have a big ball of goo.
3. Pour the meat mixture into an 8x8 glass baking dish and press down until you have an even surface through the entire dish.
4. Put in the oven for 8-10 minutes or until you see the fat rise up to the top. It won't have to be completely cooked through since you will be cooking it a second time. Once you pull it out of the oven, discard of any excess fat if you'd like. I did.
5. While the meatza is cooking, dice up the bacon and throw in a large pan over medium heat. Cook until completely cooked through and a bit crispy. Then remove with a slotted spoon and place on a plate with a paper towel to soak up excess fat. Pour the remaining excess bacon fat into a jar, leaving about 2-3 tablespoons in the pan.
6. Add the garlic clove, sweet potato and yellow onion to the pan.
7. Let the onion and sweet potato cook down for about 8-10 minutes, stirring frequently to keep from burning.
8. Once the sweet potatoes are soft and the meatza has cooked, start making layers. Add the sweet potato/onion mixture to the top of the meatza, evenly distributed. Then crack 6 eggs on top (you pick where you'd like them to go). And finally top the eggs with the bacon.
9. Place back in the oven to cook for 8-10 minutes or until eggs are cooked to your preference.
10. Let cool. Top with hot sauce because hot sauce is delightful. Eat.

- 1 pound breakfast sausage (no sugar added)
- 7 eggs (1 egg as the binder, the rest to top your meatza with)
- 6-8 slices of bacon, diced
- 1/2 sweet potato or yam, diced (the smaller, the faster it will cook)
- 1/2 yellow onion, diced
- 1 garlic clove, minced

What changes did you make?

_____

_____

_____

REAL IMPORTANT STUFF... *Kind of:*

- *If you don't like eggs over-easy or over-medium, you could make scrambled eggs instead to top it off with!*
- *You could really eat this for any meal of your day. It's that good. For reals.*

Caramelized Onion Frittata

PREP TIME: 10 MINUTES • COOK TIME: 13 MINUTES

SERVES: 4-5

- 6 eggs, whisked
- 1/2 pound Italian sausage
- 2 yellow onions, thinly sliced
- salt and pepper, to taste
- 1-2 tablespoons coconut oil (to grease the 8x8 glass baking dish)

1. Preheat oven to 350°F.
2. Cook the Italian sausage in a large skillet over medium heat until cooked through. Be sure to use a wooden spoon to break up the sausage while it cooks.
3. Place the Italian sausage in the greased, glass baking dish.
4. While pan is still hot and over medium heat, add the sliced onions to the Italian sausage grease.
5. Cook down for about 8-10 minutes, continuously stirring onions to keep them from burning.
6. While the onions are caramelizing, mix the eggs in with the Italian sausage in the baking dish.
7. Once the onions are caramelized, place the onions on top throughout the baking dish, covering all the eggs and Italian sausage.
8. Bake for 10-13 minutes or until the eggs are completely cooked through in the middle. Use the finger poke method to check!

What changes did you make?

_____

_____

_____

REAL IMPORTANT STUFF... *Kind of:*

- The more onions you caramelize, the better. Promise you.
- To make sure your eggs are cooked through, poke in the middle. If your finger sinks in, it's not done. The eggs should almost push back when you poke it. Science.

Mexican Hash Egg Bake

INGREDIENTS

PREP TIME: 10 MINUTES • COOK TIME: 10 MINUTES
SERVES: 4-6

- 1 pound chorizo (no sugar added)
- 1 (14 ounce) can diced fire-roasted tomatoes
- 1 sweet potato or yam, diced
- 1 yellow onion, diced
- 6-8 eggs
- 2 garlic cloves, minced
- 1 tablespoon fat of choice (I used bacon fat)
- 1 teaspoon smoked paprika
- 1 teaspoon garlic powder
- 1/2 teaspoon chili powder
- 1/2 teaspoon dried oregano
- salt and pepper, to taste

1. Preheat oven to 350°F.
2. Heat up a large skillet or cast iron skillet over medium heat.
3. Add the fat and minced garlic.
4. When the garlic becomes fragrant, toss in the onions, sweet potatoes and chorizo to begin to cook down.
5. Use a wooden spoon or whatever you have on hand to break up the chorizo and mix around to incorporate everything. Cover to help steam the sweet potatoes.
6. Let cook for about 6-8 minutes or until sweet potatoes are tender.
7. Add the tomatoes and spices and mix together. Now you have your hash!
8. If you are not using a cast iron skillet, pour the hash into a 9x13 glass baking dish. Otherwise, you can keep it in the skillet.
9. Use a spoon to press into the hash where you want the eggs to go.
10. Crack the eggs directly on top of hash.
11. Bake for 5-8 minutes depending how runny you want your eggs. Just press on the egg yolk with your finger to see how done it is!

What changes did you make?

_____

_____

_____

REAL IMPORTANT STUFF... *Kind of:*

- Bacon would be awesome in this. Obviously.
- The smaller you dice up your sweet potatoes, the faster they will cook, and the quicker you will eat. Genius.

Grilled Salmon and Asparagus Frittata

PREP TIME: 10 MINUTES • COOK TIME: 20 MINUTES
SERVES: 4-6

- 12 whole eggs, whisked
- 6-8 ounces salmon (or more. don't be shy.)
- 1 bundle of asparagus, ends cut off
- 1 teaspoon garlic powder
- 1 teaspoon onion powder
- 1/2 teaspoon dried thyme
- 1/2 teaspoon dried basil
- salt and pepper, to taste
- 1 tablespoon fat of choice (I used olive oil)
- aluminum foil, for the grill

1. Preheat oven to 350°F.
2. Light that grill of yours to a medium-high heat!
3. Whisk the eggs in a large bowl.
4. Salt and pepper the salmon and place on a piece of aluminum foil.
5. Place asparagus spears on a separate piece of aluminum foil and pour a tablespoon of fat over the spears and then top with salt and pepper.
6. Place both pieces of aluminum foil on the grill to cook.
7. Flip all the spears (just move them around a bit) and salmon after about 4-6 minutes to cook on the other side.
8. Do not light aluminum foil on fire, like I did.
9. Once the spears and salmon are thoroughly cooked, let cool for just a minute then roughly chop the salmon and asparagus. I cut the asparagus into thirds then took apart the salmon with my bare hands. MY BARE HANDS.
10. Throw into the bowl of whisked eggs, then add garlic and onion powders, thyme and basil, and top it all off with a bit more salt and pepper.
11. Pour into a cast iron skillet and bake for 18-20 minutes or until middle of frittata is completely cooked through.
12. Serve with something on top, like an avocado. Stupid delish.

What changes did you make?

_____

_____

_____

REAL IMPORTANT STUFF... *Kind of:*

- No fresh salmon on hand? You could also use some smoked salmon instead.
- Is asparagus like $70 per pound where you live? It's cool. Just make whatever is in season. Maybe zucchini. Maybe yellow squash. MAYBE BACON. Bacon is always in season.

INGREDIENTS

- 3/4 pound bulk breakfast sausage (no sugar added)
- 1 acorn squash, cut in half, seeds removed
- 2 eggs
- 1/2 yellow onion, diced
- 1 garlic clove, minced
- salt and pepper, to taste

Stuffed Acorn Squash

PREP TIME: 25 MINUTES • COOK TIME: 15 MINUTES

SERVES: 2

1. Preheat oven to 375°F.
2. Place acorn squash cut-side down onto the baking sheet.
3. Bake for 20-25 minutes or until the acorn squash is soft when you press on the skin.
4. Remove from oven and let cool.
5. While the acorn squash is cooking, add a tablespoon of some kind of fat to a large pan over medium heat (I used bacon fat) then add the minced garlic and diced onion.
6. Stir around to keep from burning.
7. Once the onions become translucent, add the breakfast sausage to the pan.
8. Cook down, breaking up the breakfast sausage as it cooks.
9. Once the breakfast sausage is almost all the way cooked through, turn the heat to low and add the insides of the acorn squash. Do this by using a spoon to scoop out the insides, leaving just the skin of the acorn squash. Be careful not the tear the skin!
10. Mix the acorn squash and the breakfast sausage together then add it back to the acorn squash skin
11. Once both of the acorn squash halves are full, press into the middle with a spoon to create a little resting spot for the egg.
12. Crack an egg on top.
13. Place back in the oven to cook for 10-15 minutes or until egg-cooked preference.
14. Serve!

What changes did you make?

_____

_____

_____

REAL
IMPORTANT
STUFF...
Kind of:

- *Not a fan of eggs? Or maybe your body isn't a fan of them? That's fine, just don't top it with an egg. Boom.*
- *Did you notice that this meal is only 5 ingredients, not including the salt and pepper? Pretty rad. Pretty easy. Pretty great!*

For the pancakes:
- 1 1/2 plantains, spotty in color (that means get 2 plantains that are dark brown/black in color; you will use 1 full plantain and 1/2 of the other)
- 2 eggs
- 2 tablespoons coconut flour
- 2 tablespoons canned coconut milk
- 1 heaping tablespoon sunbutter (or nutbutter)
- 1 heaping tablespoon cinnamon (or more)
- 1/2 teaspoon baking soda

- 1/2 teaspoon baking powder
- pinch of salt
- 3 tablespoons coconut oil

For the maple syrup:
- 1/2 plantain, diced
- 2 tablespoons maple syrup (or other sweetener such as coconut nectar or honey)
- 2 teaspoons cinnamon

Caramelized Plantain Pancakes

PREP TIME: 10 MINUTES • COOK TIME: 10 MINUTES
SERVES: 1-2

1. Let's caramelize these plantains. Make sure the plantains are super ripe so they are dark in color and a bit squishy. Yes, squishy. Don't squeeze too hard, that's mean.

2. Heat up a medium skillet over medium heat and add 3 tablespoons of coconut oil.

3. While the oil heats up, cut off the ends of the 2 plantains and peel back the peel. Making a slit down the side makes it quite easy to pull back.

4. Cut each plantain into three equal slices lengthwise, then place in the hot coconut oil and sprinkle with cinnamon and a bit of salt. Let cook for about 2-3 minutes per side. Once you flip them, sprinkle that side with cinnamon and a little bit of salt. Be sure not to burn them!

5. When the plantains are done cooking, remove from pan and set on a plate to cool. Leave behind 1/2 of a plantain for the syrup and place the rest of the plantains in a large bowl and use a fork to completely mash them.

6. Add the rest of the pancake ingredients to the bowl: eggs, coconut flour, coconut milk, sunbutter, cinnamon, baking soda and powder, and salt and mix well until you get a soupy paste.

7. Heat up a skillet or whatever you love to cook pancakes on. I used a non-stick skillet and added no oil to the pan and none of the pancakes stuck to the pan, but be careful.

8. Add a small amount of pancake mix to the hot skillet (I made my pancakes about 3 inches wide) and cook until bubbles begin to appear in the batter, then flip. About 2 minutes per side depending how big you make them. The smaller you make them, the easier they are to flip without breaking apart.

9. Make all of your pancakes!

10. Dice up the leftover plantains into smaller pieces and add to a bowl with the maple syrup and cinnamon.

11. Stack those pancakes, pour the syrup on top, and eat!

12. Holy crap good.

What changes did you make?

_____

_____

_____

REAL IMPORTANT STUFF... *Kind of:*

- Just because I know you totally care, I LOVE these pancakes. They are my favorite pancakes of all time. Not even kidding you.
- Not into maple syrup? What's wrong with you? My roommate's the same way. She topped hers with a bit of honey!

For the crepes:
- 3 eggs, whisked
- 1/2 cup canned coconut milk
- 2 tablespoons coconut flour
- 1 tablespoon vanilla extract
- 1 teaspoon honey

For the cherry jam:
- 1 cup cherries, seeds removed
- 2 tablespoons honey
- 1 tablespoon coconut oil
- For the whipped cream:
- 1 cup whipped coconut cream from full fat canned coconut milk*
- pinch of cinnamon
- 1/8 teaspoon vanilla extract

Cherry Jam Crepe Stack

PREP TIME: 10 MINUTES • COOK TIME: 10 MINUTES
SERVES: 1-2

1. *For the whipped cream, place a can of coconut milk (I used the Thai Kitchen coconut milk) in the refrigerator overnight and scoop out the coconut cream that has hardened in the top of the can of coconut milk, and leave the coconut water behind for something else. Like drinking, duh. Then place coconut cream in a bowl, add cinnamon and vanilla, and whip! Ta duh! Set in fridge to keep cool while you cook.

2. Put a small saucepan over medium heat and add the coconut oil and seedless cherries to the pan. Mix around to coat the cherries.

3. Let cherries begin to cook down, stirring randomly to make sure cherries don't burn or stick to the bottom of the pan.

4. While cherries are cooking, place a large skillet over medium heat.

5. Add crepe ingredients to a large bowl and whisk well to make sure coconut flour has completely broken down.

6. Once skillet is hot, add a bit of coconut oil to coat the pan (I used coconut oil spray) then pour a small amount on the skillet, about the size of the bottom of a coffee mug. Swirl the skillet around to coat the crepe around the pan so the crepe is super thin. Cook on both sides for about one minute each. Be sure to be careful when flipping the crepes; they break easily. The smaller you make them, the easier they are to flip.

7. Continue until batter is completely used up.

8. Once the cherries are soft, add the honey and mix to combine.

9. When the crepes are cooked, begin the stacking process.

10. Crepe - whipped cream - crepe - whipped cream. And so on.

11. Top with cherry jam.

12. Eat it up! Holy moly, so good!

What changes did you make?

_____

_____

_____

REAL IMPORTANT STUFF... *Kind of:*

- I suck at photography, but this picture makes me want to eat these every time I see it.
- If you prefer a savory flavor, you could make these with some savory seasonings and wrap them around breakfast sausage. Like a burrito. Or an enchilada. Beauty.

Double Chocolate Waffles

INGREDIENTS

PREP TIME: 5 MINUTES • COOK TIME: 8-10 MINUTES

SERVES: 3

- 1 1/2 cup almond meal/flour
- 1/3 cup canned coconut milk
- 1/4 cup dark chocolate chips
- 2 eggs, whisked
- 2 heaping tablespoons unsweetened cocoa powder
- 1 tablespoon maple syrup or raw honey (some kind of sweetener)
- 1 teaspoon vanilla extract
- 1/2 teaspoon baking soda
- sprinkle of cinnamon
- pinch of salt

1. Plug in your waffle iron. You don't have a waffle iron? Why not? Because it's the most pointless tool in the kitchen and takes up a ton of room? True. But buy one. Waffles are awesome. Especially paleo ones.
2. Whisk the eggs in a medium-large sized bowl.
3. Add the coconut milk and sweetener and whisk together with eggs.
4. Add the almond flour and mix more!
5. Add the cocoa powder baking soda and mix even more.
6. Add in the chocolate chips, vanilla, salt and cinnamon. Mix together thoroughly.
7. Pour into your waffle iron and bake until cooked through. It took about 4-5 minutes for mine to cook through and crisp up.

What changes did you make?

_____

_____

_____

REAL IMPORTANT STUFF...
Kind of:

- *These will change your life. If you want to get your kids, or someone stubborn, like your husband, to eat paleo, make these. They will convert anyone to the paleo lifestyle!*

100

CHOCOLATE BANANA
Breakfast Bars

PREP TIME: 10 MINUTES • COOK TIME: 25 MINUTES

SERVES: 6-8

INGREDIENTS

- 8 dried dates, pitted
- 2 bananas, peeled
- 1/3 cup sunflower seed butter (or other nut/seed butter)
- 1/4 cup protein powder (your choice)
- 2 eggs
- 3 tablespoons unsweetened cocoa powder
- 2 tablespoons ground flax seed
- 1 tablespoon coconut flour
- 1 tablespoon cinnamon
- 1 teaspoon vanilla extract
- pinch of salt

1. Preheat oven to 350°F.
2. Place the pitted dates into your food processor and puree until they begin to break down and clump together.
3. Add the banana, sunflower seed butter, vanilla extract, and eggs into your food processor, then puree.
4. Add the protein powder, flax seed, coconut flour, cinnamon and salt and puree one last time to thoroughly mix.
5. Grease an 8x8 glass baking dish and pour the mixture into the dish, smoothing out the top.
6. Place in oven for 20-25 minutes or until you poke the center of the dish with a toothpick and it comes out clean.
7. Let cool. Then cut into breakfast bar sizes, whatever that size may be to you.
8. Take on the go with you and be satisfied!

What changes did you make?

_____

_____

_____

REAL IMPORTANT STUFF...
Kind of:

- *I made these so people could have an easy-to-pack protein filled breakfast. These bars will keep you full and satisfied all morning.*
- *I love chocolate and bananas. They were created to be in a serious relationship.*

INGREDIENTS

For the waffles:
- 1 cup fresh blueberries
- 1/4 cup coconut flour
- 4 eggs
- 2 tablespoons coconut oil, melted
- 2 tablespoons raw honey
- 1 teaspoon vanilla extract
- 1 teaspoon cinnamon
- 1 teaspoon baking soda
- pinch of salt

For the blueberry maple compote:
- 1 cup fresh blueberries
- 1/3 cup maple syrup
- 2 tablespoons coconut oil
- 1/2 teaspoon cinnamon

Blueberry Waffles WITH BLUEBERRY MAPLE COMPOTE

PREP TIME: 10 MINUTES • COOK TIME: 10 MINUTES
SERVES: 1-2

1. Heat up your waffle iron.
2. Place the fresh blueberries in the food processor and puree until smooth.
3. Add the eggs, coconut oil, and vanilla extract to the food processor and puree.
4. Add the coconut flour, baking soda, cinnamon, and salt and puree.
5. Pour the waffle ingredients into your waffle iron and cook until slightly crispy. Mine took about 5-7 minutes.
6. While your waffles cook, place a small saucepan over medium heat.
7. Add the coconut oil and blueberries to the saucepan and begin to cook down.
8. When some of the blueberries have begun to explode and become more of a jam, add the maple syrup and cinnamon and mix well to combine.
9. Let simmer for 3 or so minutes until the compote begins to thicken.
10. When the waffles are done cooking, top with the blueberry compote and enjoy. I put even more maple syrup on mine, because I dig sugar.

What changes did you make?

_____

_____

_____

REAL
IMPORTANT
STUFF...
Kind of:

- *I love blueberries. Especially in waffle form. Why wouldn't you top blueberries with blueberries?*
- *This one time, I melted chocolate with dried blueberries and froze it. Then ate it like bark. I've got chocolate issues.*

Baked Goods

Baked goods were what made me believe paleo was possible. When I found out I could still have bread, still have muffins, and still have pie, just in a different version than I was used to, I was devoted. Which is weird because I never really baked in the first place. Oh hell yeah, I made many Funfetti cakes in my day. And ate more cookie dough than should be possible in someone's lifetime, but making my own baked goods from scratch seemed tedious. And boring.

It wasn't until paleo came along that I started baking like an adorable little housewife. Minus the wife... and house part. Adorable? Oh hells yeah.

If you have boyfriends or girlfriends or children or in-laws who think paleo is lamesauce... you'll definitely change their mind when you make them blueberry muffins. Or banana bread.

But be careful who you feed these things to; people don't tend to leave you alone once you feed them. And they expect you to feed them regularly. Hence why I am still single. I refuse to feed anyone who expects it from me. Selfish human beings, you are.

HERE'S WHAT'S ON THE

Menu

Baked goods?! Life is good again:

APPLE CINNAMON MUFFINS

SIMPLE BLUEBERRY MUFFINS

MAPLE WALNUT SWEET POTATO LOAF

BANANA BREAD FRENCH TOAST

BLUEBERRY AND CHOCOLATE CHIP
PUMPKIN LOAF

MAPLE BACON PECAN PUMPKIN SPICE
DONUTS

Apple Cinnamon Muffins

PREP TIME: 5 MINUTES • COOK TIME: 25-30 MINUTES

SERVES: 9

- 1 apple, cored and diced
- 1 cup almond flour/meal
- 3 tablespoons coconut flour
- 3 eggs, whisked
- 1/4 cup coconut oil, melted
- 2 tablespoons raw honey
- 1 heaping tablespoon cinnamon (the more the better)
- 1/2 teaspoon baking soda
- pinch of salt

1. Preheat oven to 350°F.
2. Add almond flour, coconut flour, cinnamon, baking soda and salt to large bowl, mix together.
3. Add eggs, oil, honey, and diced apples.
4. Mix thoroughly.
5. Place silicone liners in muffin tins, then place batter evenly throughout. The mix gave me 9 muffins.
6. Bake for 25-30 minutes. These guys take a bit of time, but they are totally worth it!
7. Let cool. Then eat them. They're just heavenly.

What changes did you make?

_____

_____

_____

REAL IMPORTANT STUFF...
Kind of:

- Not sure what the hell silicone liners are? No worries. The search engine on the Internet can be hard to figure out at times. Just use regular paper muffin liners. They do the job just fine.
- Be sure to refrigerate these guys. No preservatives make it easy for them to spoil.

Simple Blueberry Muffins

PREP TIME: 5 MINUTES • COOK TIME: 15-20 MINUTES

SERVES: 10

- 1 cup almond butter
- 1 cup almond flour/meal
- 3 eggs, whisked
- 1/2 cup honey
- 1/3 cup unsweetened shredded coconut
- 1/3 cup coconut oil, melted
- 1/2 teaspoon baking soda
- 1/2 teaspoon baking powder
- 1/4 teaspoon sea salt
- pinch of cinnamon
- 1/2 cup fresh blueberries

1. Preheat oven to 350°F.
2. Mix all ingredients together in a bowl. If you're good at baking, you'll know to mix the dry first, then the wet ingredients, then mix together, but I do all the ingredients together and it works out just fine.
3. Place ingredients into 8-10 silicone muffin liners or paper muffin liners in a muffin tin.
4. Bake for 15-20 minutes. Just keep an eye on them. They will puff up and look adorable.
5. Eat them and be happy. And merry.

What changes did you make?

_____

_____

_____

REAL IMPORTANT STUFF...
Kind of:

- *These are the most popular muffins on my website. 53 happy reviews can't be wrong!*
- *Be sure to refrigerate these guys. No preservatives make it easy for them to spoil. You can reheat them in the toaster oven.*

MAPLE WALNUT *Sweet Potato Loaf*

INGREDIENTS

PREP TIME: 40 MINUTES • COOK TIME: 18 MINUTES

SERVES: 6-8

For the bread:
- 1 medium sweet potato (or yam), equivalent to 1 cup pureed, skin removed after baking
- 1 cup roasted, unsalted cashews
- 6 medjool dates, pitted
- 3 eggs, whisked
- 2 tablespoons raw honey
- 1 teaspoon cinnamon
- 1/2 teaspoon nutmeg
- 1 teaspoon vanilla extract
- 1/4 teaspoon baking soda
- pinch of salt

For the topping:
- 1 1/2 cup walnuts, chopped
- 1/4 cup raw honey
- 2 teaspoons cinnamon
- 1 teaspoon maple extract
- pinch of salt
- 1 tablespoon coconut oil

1. Preheat oven to 425°F.
2. Using a fork, poke holes in the sweet potato and bake for 30-40 minutes or until soft and completely cooked through.
3. While the sweet potato cooks, add the dates to a food processor and pulse to break down. Then add the cashews and let run until you have a paste, with the cashews completely broken down and combined with the dates.
4. Once the sweet potato is cooked, reduce oven temperature to 350°F.
5. Add cashew and date mixture to a bowl, along with the baked sweet potato with the skin removed, eggs and all other bread ingredients. Mix well.
6. Grease two bread pans (I used 9.3 x 5.2 sized) and divide the sweet potato mixture equally between both pans.
7. Bake for 15-18 minutes then let cool.
8. While the bread is baking, place a small skillet over medium heat and add the coconut oil then chopped walnuts.
9. Let the walnuts begin to toast for a minute or two, then add the honey, cinnamon, maple extract, and pinch of salt.
10. Mix to combine and let cook for about 1-2 minutes more.
11. Add the sticky nut mixture to the top of the sweet potato breads.
12. Let cool completely (the nut mixture will harden a bit), then cut and serve!

What changes did you make?

_____

_____

_____

REAL IMPORTANT STUFF... *Kind of:*

- *Other kinds of dates will work, but medjool is just way cooler to say.*
- *No walnuts? It's cool. Any other nut or seed will do!!*

BLUEBERRY AND CHOCOLATE CHIP
Pumpkin Loaf

PREP TIME: 5 MINUTES • COOK TIME: 15-20 MINUTES

SERVES: 10

INGREDIENTS

- 1 medium banana (the browner, the better)
- 1/4 cup pureed pumpkin
- 1/4 cup blueberries
- 1/8 cup dark chocolate chips
- 1 1/2 cups roasted, unsalted cashews
- 1 cup almond meal/flour
- 2 tablespoons walnut oil
- 2 eggs, whisked
- 1 tablespoon raw honey
- 1 teaspoon baking soda
- 1 teaspoon baking powder
- 1 teaspoon vanilla extract
- 1/2 teaspoon cinnamon
- pinch of salt

1. Preheat oven to 375°F.
2. Pull out your handy dandy food processor. Add the cashews to the food processor to grind down.
3. Once you get a fine cashew meal, add the walnut oil while your food processor is still on and process until you get a cashew butter.
4. Add the peeled banana and pureed pumpkin to your food processor with the cashews. Turn your food processor on and let combine for a minute or so until you have a soupy paste. Taste it. It's stupid delicious.
5. In a large bowl, whisk the eggs, then add the cashew mixture along with almond meal/flour, baking soda and powder, honey, vanilla extract, cinnamon, and salt. Mix until you get a batter.
6. Fold in the blueberries and chocolate chips.
7. Grease a bread pan with some coconut oil. I used a loaf pan that was 9.3x5.2 inches (weird numbers) and it worked well. You could use a smaller pan for a taller loaf of bread; it just may cook differently.
8. Pour batter into the greased loaf pan. Place in oven and bake for 25-30 minutes or until bread is cooked through and the top of the loaf has a bit of a "crisp" to it.
9. Let bread cool for about 10 minutes.
10. Eat it like you mean it. Try not to eat all in one sitting. Don't say I didn't warn you.

What changes did you make?

_____

_____

_____

REAL IMPORTANT STUFF...
Kind of:

- *Pumpkins not in season where you are? Canned pumpkin is ready to go year round! Oh hells yeah!*

109

INGREDIENTS

For the bread:
- 3 medium bananas (you want them brown and spotty)
- 1 1/2 cups roasted unsalted cashews
- 1 cup almond meal/flour
- 2 tablespoons walnut oil
- 2 eggs, whisked
- 1 tablespoon raw honey
- 1 teaspoon baking soda
- 1 teaspoon baking powder
- 1 teaspoon vanilla extract
- 1/2 teaspoon cinnamon
- pinch of salt

For the French toast:
- 2 eggs, whisked
- 1/3 cup canned coconut milk
- 1 teaspoon vanilla extract
- 1/4 teaspoon cinnamon
- 1-2 tablespoons coconut oil

Banana Bread French Toast

PREP TIME: 10 MINUTES • COOK TIME: 30 MINUTES
SERVES: 2-3

1. Preheat oven to 375°F.
2. Pull out your handy dandy food processor. It will make life soooo much easier. Add the cashews to the food processor to grind down.
3. Once you get a fine cashew meal, add the walnut oil while your food processor is still on. Keep processing until you get a cashew butter.
4. Peel the bananas, roughly break them up, and add to your food processor with the cashews. Turn your food processor on and let combine for a minute or so until you have a soupy paste. A delicious soupy paste.
5. In a large bowl, whisk the eggs, then add the cashew/banana mixture along with almond meal/flour, baking soda and powder, honey, vanilla extract, cinnamon, and salt. Mix to combine until you get a batter.
6. Grease a bread pan with some coconut oil. I used a loaf pan that was 9.3x5.2 inches (weird numbers) and it worked well. You could use a smaller pan for a taller loaf of bread; it just may cook differently.
7. Pour batter into a greased loaf pan. Place in oven and bake for 25-30 minutes or until bread is cooked through and the top of the loaf has a bit of a "crisp" to it.
8. Let bread cool for about 10 minutes.
9. When banana bread has cooled, whisk together the French toast ingredients (minus the coconut oil) in a shallow bowl.
10. Heat up a skillet or griddle and add the coconut oil to it.
11. Cut the bread into 1/2-1 inch slices, dip them in the egg mixture and cover both sides, then place on griddle to cook for 2-3 minutes per side.
12. Top French toast off with sliced bananas, maple syrup or honey, and a touch of cinnamon.
13. Pure brilliance. Consume. Try to go slow. It is epic.

What changes did you make?

_____

_____

_____

REAL
IMPORTANT
STUFF...
Kind of.

• With over 300 comments on my blog and 5/5 stars from 90 reviews, I'd say this is probably one of my most popular recipes. For good reason. You can barely tell the difference from normal banana bread!

INGREDIENTS

For the donuts:
- 6 dried medjool dates, pitted
- 1/2 cup pumpkin puree
- 1/4 cup coconut oil
- 4 eggs
- 3 tablespoons coconut flour
- 1/2 tablespoon cinnamon
- 1/4 teaspoon nutmeg
- 1/8 teaspoon ground cloves
- 1/8 teaspoon ground ginger
- 1/2 teaspoon baking powder
- pinch of salt

For the topping:
- 6 strips of bacon, diced
- 1/2 cup pecans, chopped
- 1/3 cup maple syrup
- 1/4 teaspoon cinnamon
- pinch of salt

Maple Bacon Pecan Pumpkin Donuts

PREP TIME: 10 MINUTES • COOK TIME: 10 MINUTES
SERVES: 6

1. Preheat oven to 350°F.
2. Place the dried dates in a food processor and puree until you begin to get clumpy balls.
3. Add the pumpkin puree, coconut oil, and eggs and puree again.
4. Add the dry ingredients including the coconut flour, cinnamon, nutmeg, ground cloves, ground ginger, baking powder, and salt. Mix once more until combined and smooth.
5. Grease the donut pan with some extra coconut oil then pour the pumpkin donut mixture into the donut pan.
6. Bake for 20-25 minutes until the top of the donuts have a nice crust, and/or when you poke the donuts with a toothpick and it comes out clean.
7. Let cool.
8. While the donuts are baking, add the diced bacon to a medium skillet over medium heat. Cook until crispy then remove with a slotted spoon and place bacon on a plate with a paper towel to soak up the excess fat.
9. Pour extra bacon fat into a jar, leaving behind about 2 tablespoons to cook the pecans in.
10. Toss the chopped pecans into the bacon fat pan and begin to roast the pecans, moving them around frequently to make sure they do not burn.
11. When the pecans begin to brown a bit and become fragrant, add in the maple syrup, cinnamon and a bit of salt and mix to incorporate.
12. After about 2-3 minutes, when the syrup begins to thicken, remove from heat and add the crispy bacon to the pan and mix around to coat.
13. While the pecan and bacon mixture is still warm, pour onto the donuts. You'll need to press the mixture onto the donuts a little to get it to stick.
14. Let sit for about 5 minutes to let the toppings harden, then serve.
15. Eat it with coffee. Because coffee is wonderful. But donuts and coffee are even better.

What changes did you make?

_____

_____

_____

REAL IMPORTANT STUFF... *Kind of:*

• *These donuts rocked my world. No need to eat any other kind after trying these. So do it. Try them.*

5 Ingredient
MEALS

Some of these recipes may seem like they have six ingredients in them. That's because they do. But one of the ingredients is salt and pepper most of the time. And if you're complaining about one extra ingredient, then omit your salt and pepper. Be boring. And less flavorful. Your pallet is yours. Your life is yours. Your boringness is yours.

I created these recipes mainly for bachelors. Yes, I know all kinds of people out there like simple meals, but more often than not, my man friends and man blog readers complain that my meals are too complicated. Are you kidding me? They are not that damn hard. If I created them, seriously, anybody can make them. Man up, bro.

But what I have found is that even though I like fancier meals when I have time to cook them, I often stick with easy-to-assemble meals. Like sardines with avocado and a little salt. The tin can has already created a bowl for you. No clean up. GENIUS.

But if you don't like these recipe ideas, try some of these combinations:

1. Bacon + Eggs + Sweet potatoes
2. Chicken Sausage + Roasted Broccoli + Hot Sauce
3. Shredded Pork + Avocado
4. Steak + Peppers + Salsa
5. Italian Sausage + Zucchini + Yellow Squash
6. Burger. It's as simple as that.

HERE'S WHAT'S ON THE

Menu

7 simple meals to keep you satis-fied, without wasting your time:

AVOCADO PUDDING

BANGERS AND MASH

QUICK SPAGHETTI

BREAKFAST IN A PINCH

SLOW-COOKED SALSA CHICKEN

SWEET POTATO SNACK

SAVORY STEAK AND MUSHROOMS

Avocado Pudding

PREP TIME: 5 MINUTES

SERVES: 1

- 1/2 avocado, mashed
- 1-2 tablespoons unsweetened cocoa powder (the more, the chocolatey-er)
- 2 teaspoons raw honey
- 1 teaspoon sunflower seed butter (or other nut butter)
- pinch of salt
- dark chocolate chips (optional)

1. Mash up the avocado.
2. Add in the cocoa powder, raw honey, sunbutter, pinch of salt and mix thoroughly.
3. Top with dark chocolate chips if you would like. I liked.
4. Eat it up!

What changes did you make?

_____

_____

_____

REAL IMPORTANT STUFF... *Kind of:*

- *If you want over-the-top chocolatey flavor and a protein boost, add a tablespoon of your favorite chocolate protein powder!*
- *For an even smoother pudding, place all ingredients in the food processor! Then you won't have any green chunks that creep you or your guests out.*

116

Bangers and Mash

INGREDIENTS

PREP TIME: 10 MINUTES • COOK TIME: 40 MINUTES

SERVES: 2-4

- 4 pork sausages (or any sausage on sale!!)
- 2 yellow onions, peeled and sliced
- 1 butternut squash, peeled and diced (seeds removed)
- 2 tablespoons garlic powder
- 4 tablespoons olive oil
- salt and pepper, to taste

1. Preheat oven to 400°F.
2. Place the diced butternut squash in a 9x12 glass baking dish, pour 2 tablespoons of olive oil over the squash then sprinkle 2 tablespoons garlic powder on top along with a bit of salt and pepper. Use your hands or a large spoon to mix the oil with the squash.
3. Bake for 35-40 minutes.
4. Once you get the squash in the oven, pull out another large glass baking dish.
5. Place the sausages and sliced onions in the baking dish and pour 2 tablespoons of olive oil on top then sprinkle garlic powder, salt and pepper on top.
6. When the squash has about 20 minutes left to cook, put the sausage and onion baking dish into the oven next to the squash and cook for 20 minutes, or until cooked through.
7. Once the two dishes are done baking, place the butternut squash in a food processor to puree.
8. Place the pureed squash mash in a bowl, top it off with the sausages and caramelized onions. The burnt ones are the best. Fact.

What changes did you make?

_____

_____

_____

REAL IMPORTANT STUFF... *Kind of:*

- *Only have 1 baking dish? Oh that's fine! Just bake your squash first, then bake your onions and sausage at the same temperature. Your squash will hold its heat!*
- *No food processor? You dummy, go buy one. But in the mean time, use a fork to mash up your squash instead.*

Quick Spaghetti

PREP TIME: 25 MINUTES • COOK TIME: 10 MINUTES

SERVES: 3-4

- 1 pound Italian sausage
- 1 cup tomato sauce
- 1 medium spaghetti squash, halved lengthwise, excess seeds removed
- 2 teaspoons garlic powder
- salt and pepper, to taste

1. Preheat oven to 400°F.
2. Place the halved spaghetti squash open-side down on a baking sheet.
3. Bake for 20-25 minutes or until spaghetti squash is soft to the touch when you poke the skin.
4. When spaghetti squash is almost done cooking, add the Italian sausage to a medium pan and over medium heat.
5. Break up sausage with a wooden spoon.
6. Once the sausage has almost cooked through, add the tomato sauce, garlic powder, and salt and pepper to taste.
7. When the sausage is done cooking and the sauce is nice and hot, use a fork to pull the threads from the spaghetti squash and place the threads into the pan.
8. Mix well.
9. Eat!!

What changes did you make?

_____

_____

_____

REAL IMPORTANT STUFF... *Kind of:*

- *In quick dishes like this, the more seasonings and spices you use, the more delicious the food will be. If you have parsley, oregano, and basil on hand, add it!*
- *No tomato sauce? Diced tomatoes would work as well!*

Breakfast In A Pinch

PREP TIME: 5 MINUTES • COOK TIME: 10 MINUTES

SERVES: 1

INGREDIENTS

- 3 eggs
- 1/3 pound bulk breakfast sausage
- 1/2 sweet potato, diced
- 1 poblano pepper, seeds removed, diced
- 1 garlic clove, minced
- salt and pepper, to taste

1. Place a large pan over medium heat and add a tablespoon of your choice of fat. Bacon fat is the best. Fact.
2. Add minced garlic then the sweet potato and poblano.
3. Add a tablespoon of water, then cover to help the sweet potato cook quicker.
4. When the sweet potatoes have begun to brown, add the bulk sausage to the pan and break up with a wooden spoon.
5. Once the breakfast sausage is cooked through, crack the eggs directly into the pan, salt and pepper the ingredients, and use a spoon to break it all up and cook the eggs.
6. Once eggs are fully cooked, remove from heat and eat up. You could even eat it from the pan if you wanted to. No dishes mean a happier life.

What changes did you make?

_____

_____

_____

REAL IMPORTANT STUFF...
Kind of:

- *Make sure your breakfast sausage isn't stuffed with weird sugars.*
- *I came up with this dish one time when I was cooking for my friend Tom who makes my apparel and helps me create cooking videos. He pretty much takes care of me so I cook for him. Fantastic friendship if you ask me.*

119

Slow-Cooked Salsa Chicken

PREP TIME: 5 MINUTES • COOK TIME: 6-8 HOURS

SERVES: 3-4

- 1 whole chicken
- 2 yellow onions, sliced
- 1 cup chicken broth (no sugar added)
- 3 garlic cloves, minced
- 1/3 cup salsa (your favorite kind - no sugar added)
- salt and pepper, to taste

1. Place the sliced onions, then the whole chicken in a slow cooker.
2. Pour in the chicken broth.
3. Toss in the minced garlic cloves and salsa.
4. Top off with salt and pepper.
5. Let cook for 6-8 hours on low.
6. Use a fork to pick off the chicken and pull some of the onions from the bottom of the slow cooker.
7. Eat up and enjoy the simple chicken life.

What changes did you make?

_____

_____

_____

REAL IMPORTANT STUFF... *Kind of:*

- *This chicken will fall off the bone, so use tongs to pull off the chicken and pour some of the salsa juice on top.*
- *Be careful, this chicken will be HOT. I almost lost a mouth experimenting with this recipe.*

120

Sweet Potato Protein Snack

PREP TIME: 30 MINUTES • COOK TIME: 10 MINUTES

SERVES: 1

- 1 sweet potato or yam
- 1/3 cup canned coconut milk
- 2 tablespoons almond butter
- 1 scoop protein powder
- 1/4 teaspoon cinnamon
- pinch of salt

1. Preheat oven to 400°F.
2. Poke holes in the sweet potato all over with a fork.
3. Bake for 30-35 minutes or until soft.
4. When the sweet potato is almost done cooking, add the coconut milk to a saucepan along with the almond butter, protein powder, cinnamon, and a pinch of salt. Mix until well combined.
5. Once the sweet potato is done cooking, remove the skin, place sweet potato in a bowl, pour the mixture over the sweet potato, then mash it all together.
6. Eat right there or take on the go. Best. snack.ever.

What changes did you make?

_____

_____

_____

REAL IMPORTANT STUFF...
Kind of:

- *No nuts for you? Try using sunflower seed butter instead!*
- *This is an awesome post-workout snack. Lots of carbs and protein to refuel you. Yay for working out and eating!*

- 1/2 pound steak, chopped (your favorite cut)
- 2 cups oyster mushrooms
- 3 tablespoons fat of choice (I used bacon fat)
- 2 garlic cloves, minced
- 1-2 teaspoons dried basil
- salt and pepper, to taste

Savory Steak and Mushrooms

PREP TIME: 5 MINUTES • COOK TIME: 10 MINUTES
SERVES: 1-2

1. Place a medium skillet over medium heat.
2. Add the fat to the pan and toss in the minced garlic.
3. Throw in the mushrooms and a bit of salt to sauté.
4. When the mushrooms begin to brown, move them to the outside of the pan, and add the steak to the middle of the pan. Sprinkle with salt and pepper.
5. Let the steak sear on one side and get a nice crust, then flip.
6. Once the steak is cooked to preference, sprinkle with dried basil and serve!
7. Holy moly that was easy! I even made this dish at five in the morning, while doing my hair and makeup. Multitasking if I ever saw it.

What changes did you make?

_____

_____

_____

REAL IMPORTANT STUFF... *Kind of.*

- *If you can't find oyster mushrooms, any kind would do! Like shitake. Those are quite amazing.*
- *Choose any steak that suits your fancy. And to make your life even easier, ask the butcher to dice it up for you!*

Side Dishes

II don't really respect side dishes as much as I should. If you've read my blog before, you know I don't post many side dishes. That's because my side dishes usually include a jar of coconut butter and a spoon. Rarely do I add in vegetables to my meal if they are not already in the dish. Call it lazy. Call it unhealthy. I call it smart. Sometimes the only thing I want in life is some protein and fat. I'm just a simple girl.

That's the thing about me, I like my meals pretty simple most of the time. And my friends. That's probably why many of my friends are people from the gym I work at. Most gym people are simple and like-minded. Most. So during the summer, us like-minded-heavy-lifting friends get together on my back porch, consume far more protein than needed, and drink beverages that aren't exactly paleo-friendly. That's the beautiful thing about paleo, you get to make paleo your own happy diet. My diet includes steak and gluten free ciders on a Friday night. Yes, plural.

So when you're wondering what you're going to eat at your friend's BBQ, relax. Have a beer. Then see who can do the dumbest things in the shortest amount of time. Now that's a good Friday night.

124

HERE'S WHAT'S ON THE

Menu

*Because an entrée can get real
lonely sometimes:*

BROCCOLI FRITTERS

CINNAMON BACON BACKYARD SWEET POTATOES

BACON PECAN BRUSSELS SPROUTS

SWEET-CURRIED CAULIFLOWER SOUP

APPLE AND JICAMA SALAD

ROASTED GRAPE, BACON AND KALE SALAD

ROASTED GARLIC MASHED POTATOES

MOLÉ MEXICAN RICE

Broccoli Fritters

INGREDIENTS

PREP TIME: 10 MINUTES • COOK TIME: 10 MINUTES

SERVES: 2-4

- 6-7 broccoli stems, shredded (about 1 1/2 to 2 cups)
- 2 eggs, whisked
- 1 3/4 cup almond meal
- 1/2 sweet onion, finely chopped
- 1 tablespoon garlic powder
- 1 teaspoon minced garlic
- lots of salt and pepper
- 1-2 tablespoons fat of choice (I used bacon fat)

1. Send the broccoli stems through a shredder. I used a food processor with the shredding attachment which made it go by super fast. But you could also use a cheese grater.
2. Add the shredded broccoli stems to a large bowl along with all other ingredients and mix well.
3. Heat up a large skillet over medium-high heat with a bit of fat in it. Use a large spoon and your hands to ball up a fritter and add to a skillet. It doesn't need to be flat, you'll flatten it out after you flip it.
4. Cook the fritter for about 3-4 minutes, then use a spatula to flip, and then flatten it out with the spatula. Cook for another 4 minutes or so.
5. Once the fritters are crisp on both sides, eat them. I topped mine with a grass fed beef burger. Genius.

What changes did you make?

_____

_____

_____

REAL IMPORTANT STUFF...
Kind of:

- *Don't have just broccoli stems sitting around? Use the whole broccoli!*
- *Want even more flavor? Add some fresh herbs to your fritters!*

CINNAMON BACON
Backyard Sweet Potatoes

PREP TIME: 10 MINUTES • COOK TIME: 10 MINUTES

SERVES: 2-4

INGREDIENTS

- 2 long skinny sweet potatoes or yams (to keep the slices the same size), thinly sliced (about 1/8-1/4 inch)
- 4 pieces of bacon, diced
- 1/2-1 teaspoon cinnamon
- sprinkle of salt
- 2 large pieces of aluminum foil

1. Turn on your grill to a medium heat.
2. Lay out a large piece of aluminum.
3. Sprinkle a couple pieces of bacon on the foil. This will help the sweet potatoes from sticking.
4. Place sweet potatoes on top and spread out evenly. It's fine if they overlap, it doesn't have to be perfect. They will all cook.
5. Sprinkle with cinnamon, salt, and add the rest of the bacon on top.
6. Slightly curl up the sides of the foil, place a smaller piece of foil on top, then lock in all the sides around the foil. Like a little package. Or packet. Whatever.
7. Place on top rack of grill and let cook for about 25-30 minutes or until they are cooked completely through and soft. If you place it on the main part of the grill (I don't know grill terms) they will cook quicker, but will be more likely burn a bit.

What changes did you make?

_____

_____

_____

REAL IMPORTANT STUFF...
Kind of:

- *No grill? Or backyard? I got you. Try cooking in the oven at 350 degrees for 25-30 minutes.*
- *Want to go a spicier route? Try sprinkling with hot sauce. One of my readers did that. Told you I have the best readers.*

Bacon Pecan Brussels Sprouts

PREP TIME: 10 MINUTES • COOK TIME: 10 MINUTES

SERVES: 2-4

- 1/2 pound Brussels sprouts, halved
- 6 ounces bacon, diced
- 1/2 cup pecans
- salt and pepper, to taste

1. Preheat oven to 375°F.
2. Cut off the end of the Brussels sprouts then cut each one in half.
3. Throw the diced bacon in a large skillet over medium heat and cook until it begins to brown.
4. Add the pecans to roast with the bacon in the bacon fat.
5. Once bacon is fully cooked, remove bacon and pecans with a slotted spoon and put in a bowl.
6. Add Brussels sprouts directly to the bacon fat pan, add some salt and pepper, and cover to let cook for a bit. About 6 minutes or so.
7. Once the Brussels sprouts are browned a bit on the outside, either add that pan directly to the oven or transfer the sprouts to a baking dish then put in the oven for roasting.
8. Leave in the oven for about 20-25 minutes, adding the bacon and pecans back to the Brussels sprouts after about 15 minutes to finish cooking all together.
9. Let cool a bit, then eat.

What changes did you make?

_____

_____

_____

REAL IMPORTANT STUFF... *Kind of.*

- *No pecans? Use walnuts!*
- *I made this as a dish for Thanksgiving two years ago, never having eaten Brussels sprouts before. So happy I tried them, they have changed my love for greens!*

Sweet Curried Cauliflower Soup

INGREDIENTS

PREP TIME: 10 MINUTES • COOK TIME: 10 MINUTES
SERVES: 2-4

- 1 head of cauliflower, roughly chopped
- 1 sweet onion, chopped
- 1 apple, cored and chopped
- 1 garlic clove, minced
- 1/2 can coconut milk
- 2 cups chicken broth (or veggie broth)
- 2 tablespoons curry powder
- 1 tablespoon raw honey
- 1 tablespoon garlic powder
- 1-2 teaspoons salt
- 1/8 teaspoon cinnamon
- dash of black pepper
- 1-2 tablespoons olive oil

1. Preheat oven to 400°F.
2. Clean off the cauliflower and roughly chop into florets. Pour just a little olive oil on top with a bit of salt. Roast for about 20 minutes.
3. While the cauliflower is roasting, pull out a soup pot and add a little bit of olive oil to it over medium heat.
4. Add the minced garlic. Once the room is fragrant, add chopped onions and apples. Once they've begun to sweat (I love that term), add the chicken broth and coconut milk.
5. Add the spices and honey.
6. Simmer under low heat for around 5-8 minutes.
7. Now add everything to your immersion blender or food processor (like I did). I had to do mine in two separate batches so it didn't overflow.
8. Add a little dollop of honey on top. Add meat if you're smart. Or don't. It's your food.
9. Consume!

What changes did you make?

_____

_____

_____

REAL IMPORTANT STUFF...
Kind of:

- *Want to spice this dish up and keep yourself fuller, longer? Add cooked hot Italian sausage. Promise you, you will not regret that decision.*
- *No cauliflower? Try using butternut squash instead. Apple and butternut squash are beautiful together.*

Apple and Jicama Salad

PREP TIME: 10 MINUTES

SERVES: 2-3

- 1 apple, cored and diced
- 1 jicama, skin removed, diced
- 1 tablespoon Dijon mustard
- 1 tablespoon olive oil
- 1 teaspoon white wine vinegar
- 2 tablespoons fresh basil, chopped
- 1 tablespoon dried parsley
- pinch of salt

1. Add all ingredients to a bowl.
2. Mix well.
3. Consume.
4. That was easy. And delicious. Paleo is wonderful.

What changes did you make?

_____

_____

_____

REAL IMPORTANT STUFF... *Kind of:*

- Keep this salad chilled to make sure it stays extra crunchy.
- Want even more flavor in this dish? Add fresh herbs and don't be shy with them!

Roasted Grape, Bacon, and Kale Salad

PREP TIME: 20 MINUTES • COOK TIME: 10 MINUTES

SERVES: 3-4

- 1 bundle of kale, roughly chopped (equivalent to 5-6 cups chopped)
- 1 cup red, seedless grapes
- 5-6 strips of bacon, diced
- salt and pepper, to taste
- 2 tablespoons olive oil
- 1 tablespoon balsamic vinegar

1. Preheat oven to 425°F.
2. Place red grapes on a baking sheet and pour the olive oil and balsamic vinegar over the grapes, along with a sprinkle of salt.
3. Bake for 15-20 minutes or until grapes begin to split a little.
4. When the grapes have about 8 or so minutes left, add the diced bacon to a large skillet over medium heat.
5. Break up bacon and cook on both sides until crispy. Use a slotted spoon to remove bacon from the skillet and place on a paper towel to soak up the excess fat.
6. With 3 or so tablespoons of bacon fat left behind, toss in the roughly chopped kale and cover. Let kale cook down, tossing kale to make sure it does not burn. Cook kale for 5-6 minutes then remove from heat.
7. In a bowl, pour in the roasted grapes along with kale and bacon, and toss. Sprinkle with salt and pepper, then serve!

What changes did you make?

_____

_____

_____

REAL IMPORTANT STUFF... *Kind of.*

- *This dish is perfect on a cold night with a perfectly good steak. You know how I know that? Because that's how I ate it.*
- *A nice crunch would be perfect for this salad. Add some roasted chopped walnuts to the dish!*

Roasted Garlic-Mashed Potatoes

PREP TIME: 10 MINUTES • COOK TIME: 10 MINUTES

SERVES: 4

INGREDIENTS

- 1 head of cauliflower, leaves and stem removed
- 1 head of garlic
- 1 tablespoon olive oil
- 2-3 tablespoons canned coconut milk
- salt and pepper

1. Preheat oven to 400°F.
2. Chop up the cauliflower into smaller florets and place in a large baking dish to roast.
3. You'll also need to roast the garlic, so cut off the end of the head of garlic to show the clover. Sprinkle a bit of olive oil on the head of garlic then wrap foil around it.
4. Place the cauliflower and foil packet in the oven to bake for about 30-35 minutes.
5. Once everything is roasted away, remove from oven.
6. Place roasted cauliflower in your wonderful food processor along with roasted garlic cloves. To get the cloves from the head of garlic, just squeeze them out or use a fork to pull them out. I just took the head of garlic and squeezed the crap out of it, into my food processor.
7. Turn food processor on, pulse until garlic and cauliflower begin to become a paste, then add olive oil and coconut milk to help form your preferred texture. If you want it a bit smoother, add a little more coconut milk. Just play it by ear.
8. Add salt and pepper to taste.
9. Consume. I ate mine with a bacon wrapped steak. Fantastic.

What changes did you make?

_____

_____

_____

REAL IMPORTANT STUFF... *Kind of.*

- *Don't be afraid to add more roasted garlic to these. Garlic makes everything better. Except for brownies. That's just weird.*
- *The more you puree your cauliflower, the smoother it will become. Don't be afraid to add butter, if you're into that. I do that sometimes. It makes me feel naughty, which is fun.*

Molé Mexican Rice

PREP TIME: 10 MINUTES • COOK TIME: 15 MINUTES

SERVES: 2-3

INGREDIENTS

- 1 head of cauliflower, leaves and stem removed
- 1/2 yellow onion, finely diced
- 1 yellow pepper, diced
- 2 tablespoons olive oil
- 2 garlic cloves, minced
- 1/2 cup vegetable broth
- 4 ounce tomato paste
- 2-3 ounces 90% dark chocolate, roughly chopped
- 1 tablespoon unsweetened cocoa powder
- 1 teaspoon cumin
- 1/2 teaspoon dried oregano
- 1/4 teaspoon red pepper flakes
- salt and pepper, to taste
- 2 tablespoons cacao nibs (optional)
- 2 tablespoons fat of choice (I used bacon fat)
- chopped green onions, to garnish

1. Pull out your food processor so you can rice the cauliflower.
2. Roughly chop the cauliflower and place it in the food processor with the shredding attachment to create the rice.
3. Place a medium saucepan over medium heat and add 2 tablespoons of fat and minced garlic.
4. Once the garlic becomes fragrant, add the diced onion.
5. Add the cauliflower to begin to cook down. After about 3-4 minutes, add the broth to the rice. Mix well and cover.
6. Melt the chocolate.
7. After about 5-8 minutes, add the tomato paste, chocolate, cocoa powder, and spices, and combine.
8. Once it is mixed thoroughly, turn the burner down low and let it simmer for about 5-8 minutes, stirring occasionally to make sure it does not stick to the bottom.
9. When the rice is all cooked through and has become thick and sticky, put it on a plate, sprinkle with cacao nibs, and top with chopped green onions.

What changes did you make?

_____

_____

_____

REAL IMPORTANT STUFF...
Kind of:

- *This dish is perfect on a cold night with a perfectly good steak. You know how I know that? Because that's how I ate it.*
- *A nice crunch would be perfect for this salad. Add some roasted chopped walnuts to the dish!*

133

Snacks

Look at that. Who needs human interaction when appliance-love goes even deeper. I freaking love my food processor. It's the appliance I use the most in my kitchen. You can puree, you can chop, you can shred, you can slice. Pretty much the only thing you can't do with your food processor is go on a date with it. Believe me, I've tried. You should have seen the stares I received while I walked through the park with my food processor during my photo shoot for the cookbook. People hate weird people. Thank gosh I embrace it.

Embracing our own personal weirdness is what leads us to meeting even weirder people than ourselves. Like my best guy friend, Sergio. If you've ever read my blog, you know I mention him often. And you know that he is probably the most hilarious person in this world. That being said, he's weird as hell. Not everyone can handle some of the things that come out of his mouth. I'm surprised I even can. All he does is make fun of me, my large bum, and how much I talk about myself on my blog. But it doesn't offend me BECAUSE I'm just as weird. And if I had never embraced my weirdness, I would have never met the most hilarious and most food-loving person out there. Of course, second to me. Obviously.

So here's my advice to you, because I know you so want it. Be yourself, because no matter how weird you are, someone out there is just as weird as you are. And if you hide that weirdness, you may never meet those sons of b*tches that make you laugh until you pee yourself. I'm not even kidding you, he's made me do that.

Can my jeans be any tighter? My goodness, those look like spandex for gosh sakes. That seems to be what Olympic lifting leads to. Spandex-looking jeans. Yeah, that's it. It's not my choice in jeans at all. AT ALL.

134

HERE'S WHAT'S ON THE

Menu

Now you'll never have an excuse to not have a delicious snack!

CHUNKY PINEAPPLE GUACAMOLE WITH GRILLED SWEET POTATO CHIPS

SPINACH AND ARTICHOKE DIP WITH BAKED PLANTAIN CHIPS

BABY PIZZA BITES

ROASTED RED PEPPER DIP WITH BAKED SWEET POTATO CHIPS

DOUBLE CHOCOLATE ENERGY BITES

PUMPKIN GRANOLA

BACON SWEET POTATO POUTINE

HERB CARROT FRIES WITH ROASTED GARLIC DIP

HOMEMADE HONEY CINNAMON ALMOND BUTTER

SMOKED SALMON DEVILED EGGS

CUBAN TURKEY ROLL UPS

PUMPKIN PIE APPLE DIP

Chunky Pineapple Guacamole
WITH GRILLED SWEET POTATO CHIPS

PREP TIME: 5 MINUTES • COOK TIME: 15-20 MINUTES
SERVES: 2-3

INGREDIENTS

- 2 avocados, cut in half, pits removed
- 1/2 pineapple, diced
- 1 skinny yam or sweet potato, sliced thin into chips
- 1/2 jalapeño, finely diced
- 1/4 red onion, finely diced
- 2-3 tablespoons cilantro, diced
- 2 garlic cloves, finely diced
- 1 teaspoon granulated garlic
- 1/2 teaspoon cayenne pepper
- salt and pepper, to taste
- 1-2 tablespoons coconut oil, melted
- aluminum foil

1. Heat up your grill to a low heat.
2. Place sliced sweet potatoes on aluminum foil and use a brush to brush on some coconut oil on each sweet potato and top off with some salt.
3. Place on grill to cook. You will need to flip them after about 8-10 minutes depending on how hot your grill is. I kept the temperature down low to avoid burning the chips.
4. While the sweet potatoes cook, add the insides of the avocados to a large bowl and use a fork to mash up the avocado.
5. Add the pineapple, jalapeño, red onion, garlic, cilantro, spices, salt and pepper to the avocados.
6. Mix thoroughly.
7. Once the sweet potato chips have charred a bit and cooled on a piece of a paper towel, start dipping.
8. I love guac. Especially with sweetness added to it.
9. Boom.

What changes did you make?

_____

_____

_____

REAL IMPORTANT STUFF... *Kind of:*

- I've made a mango guacamole and it was just as delicious!
- No grill? Don't worry. In just a couple pages, you'll see I have a great recipe for BAKED sweet potato chips!

Spinach and Artichoke Dip

DIP WITH BAKED PLANTAIN CHIPS

PREP TIME: 10 MINUTES • COOK TIME: 15 MINUTES

SERVES: 2-3

INGREDIENTS

For the dip:

- 2 (14 ounce) cans artichoke hearts (mine were in brine), roughly chopped
- 16 ounces frozen spinach
- 1 cup cashews, roasted and unsalted
- 2 tablespoons olive oil
- 1 tablespoon garlic powder
- 1 teaspoon onion powder
- 1 teaspoon dried basil
- 1 teaspoon sea salt
- 1/2 teaspoon black pepper
- 1/4 teaspoon cayenne pepper

For the chips:

- 2 pounds plantains, peeled, and thinly sliced on the diagonal
- 1/4 cup coconut oil
- coarse salt and ground pepper

For the chips:

1. Preheat oven to 350°F.
2. Toss sliced plantains with coconut oil, then arrange in a single layer on two baking sheets.
3. Season with salt and pepper.
4. Bake for 30-35 minutes or until golden and crisp baking, flipping plantains halfway through.
5. Dry plantains on paper towels to soak up excess oil.

For the dip:

6. While the chips are baking, add frozen spinach and artichokes to large saucepan over medium heat and sprinkle with just a bit of salt.
7. While the spinach thaws and artichokes warm up, pull out your handy dandy food processor.
8. Place cashews in food processor. Grind until the cashews become a meal/flour, then begin to pour in the olive oil until you get a creamy consistency. Kind of like a super creamy cashew butter.
9. Once the spinach is completely thawed and it's all good and warm, drain the excess water from the saucepan and add the spinach and artichokes to a large bowl.
10. Add the creamy cashews and seasonings to the bowl and mix thoroughly.

What changes did you make?

_____

_____

_____

REAL IMPORTANT STUFF...
Kind of:

- *I told you I love plantains. Especially in chip form. I can't get enough of plantain chips. I sometimes, meaning all the time, buy them at the store and cannot stop eating them.*
- *If you do dairy, this recipe is AMAZING with goat cheese. Trust me.*

137

Baby Pizza Bites

PREP TIME: 8 MINUTES • COOK TIME: 10 MINUTES

SERVES: 4-6

INGREDIENTS

- 12 button mushrooms, wiped of any dirt and stems removed
- 1/2 pound Italian sausage
- 1 egg white
- 1/4-1/2 cup pizza sauce or no-sugar-added marinara sauce

1. Turn on your grill so it's hot. Makes sense.
2. Wipe down the mushrooms and remove stems. Then place them stem side up on a plate.
3. Throw the Italian sausage in a bowl along with the egg white. Use your hands to combine it all together.
4. Make tablespoon size balls of the meat mixture and plop them into the cap of the mushrooms.
5. Place on top rack of grill and cook for about 8-10 minutes or until sausage is cooked through.
6. Top each mushroom and sausage cap with either hot or cold pizza/marinara sauce!
7. Stick a toothpick in it and EAT IT.

What changes did you make?

_____

_____

_____

REAL IMPORTANT STUFF...
Kind of:

- *You ever miss pizza? I do ALL THE DAMN TIME. These are like mini pizzas. Nice trick for your taste buds.*
- *Be careful, these babies get HOT. Like burn the roof of your mouth off hot. You were warned.*

Baked Sweet Potato Chips

PREP TIME: 10 MINUTES • COOK TIME: 20 MINUTES
SERVES: 2-4

For the chips:
- 4 sweet potatoes or yams (try to grab skinny ones)
- 2-3 tablespoons coconut oil
- salt, to taste

For the dip:
- 1 (12-14 ounce) jar of roasted red peppers
- 1 cup walnuts, unsalted, chopped
- 1 garlic clove, peeled
- 1-2 teaspoons olive oil
- 1/2 teaspoon onion powder
- salt, to taste

For the chips:
1. Preheat oven to 400°F.
2. Use a mandolin or a knife to cut the sweet potatoes thin. I'd say the thickness of a silver dollar or maybe a little thicker.
3. Put some parchment paper down on a baking sheet and place sweet potato rounds on the parchment paper.
4. Melt coconut oil by placing your jar in the microwave for 30 seconds to one minute, then use a pastry/cooking brush to paint some coconut oil on top of each sweet potato round.
5. Sprinkle salt on top.
6. Place in the oven to bake for around 8-10 minutes.
7. Flip sweet potatoes over and bake for another 5 minutes or until edges are brown and have curled up a bit.
8. Let cool.

For the dip:
9. While the chips are baking, pull out your handy dandy food processor.
10. Add roasted red peppers and garlic clove. Turn on to puree.
11. Add the walnuts and turn your food processor back on to make a paste.
12. Add olive oil, onion powder, and salt. Puree until you get the consistency you like.
13. Place in fridge to chill before serving with the chips.
14. Add the creamy cashews and seasonings to the bowl and mix thoroughly.

What changes did you make?

_____

_____

_____

REAL IMPORTANT STUFF... *Kind of:*

- This dip will wow your guests. They will never know that it's paleo. Promise, swear.
- Want a spicier chip? Top them with some cayenne pepper for a little kick.

Double Chocolate Energy Bites

PREP TIME: 5 MINUTES
SERVES: 2-4

- 1 cup almond butter (or other nut/seed butter)
- 1 1/2 cups unsweetened shredded coconut
- 8-10 dried black figs, stems removed
- 1/2 cup dark chocolate chips
- 1/4 cup flaxseed meal
- 4 tablespoons raw honey
- 2 tablespoons unsweetened cocoa powder
- 1-2 scoops chocolate protein powder of choice
- 1 teaspoon vanilla extract
- pinch of salt

1. Add all ingredients to a food processor (except for the chocolate chips).
2. Turn food processor on.
3. Let ingredients mix until dried figs are completely broken down and incorporated.
4. Add mixture to a bowl and fold in chocolate chips.
5. Shape mixture into bite-sized balls.
6. Place in the refrigerator to help harden.
7. Consume.
8. Keep leftovers in the fridge!
9. Be merry.

What changes did you make?

_____

_____

_____

REAL IMPORTANT STUFF...
Kind of.

- These little guys are AWESOME. The recipe says it serves 2-4, but that's because you can't just eat one. Fact.
- I call these energy bites because these things give you more energy than you knew possible. At least they do for me. Maybe it's because I'm just really hyper.

Pumpkin Granola

INGREDIENTS

PREP TIME: 10 MINUTES • COOK TIME: 40 MINUTES

SERVES: 4-6

- 1/2 cup sliced almonds
- 1/2 cup pumpkin seeds (pepitas)
- 1/2 cup pecans, chopped
- 8-10 dried medjool dates, pits removed, roughly chopped
- 1/2 cup pumpkin puree
- 1/3 cup coconut oil, melted
- 1/3 cup unsweetened shredded coconut
- 1/3 cup maple syrup
- 1 teaspoon vanilla extract
- 2 tablespoons cinnamon
- 2 tablespoons nutmeg
- 1/8 teaspoon ground cloves
- 1/8 teaspoon ground ginger
- pinch of salt

1. Preheat oven to 325°F.
2. In a large mixing bowl, add the pumpkin puree, coconut oil, maple syrup, vanilla extract, and all spices. Mix well.
3. Add the nuts, seeds, and dates and mix well with the wet ingredients.
4. Line parchment paper on a large baking sheet and pour the granola mixture on top. Use a spoon to spread out the mixture evenly so everything will cook at the same time.
5. Place in oven and cook for 30-40 minutes, moving the granola around half way through to be sure it doesn't burn.
6. LET COOL. Letting the granola cool will help it to harden, and that's what you want from granola. Duh.
7. Eat all by itself or top it off with coconut milk, almond milk, or even dairy milk (if you do that).
8. Enjoy the paleo life. It's beautiful.

What changes did you make?

_____

_____

_____

REAL IMPORTANT STUFF...
Kind of:

- *You'll never miss normal granola or cereal again. This granola is like eating the real thing!*
- *If you like hiking, unlike me, this is a perfect on-the-go snack. Or if you're like me, this is the perfect snack to eat while sitting at a coffee shop, blogging.*

INGREDIENTS

- 1 sweet potato or yam, cut lengthwise into french fries (per your preference)
- 6-8 strips of bacon, cut into 1 inch pieces
- 1 head of cauliflower, stem removed, cut into small florets
- 1/2 cup canned coconut milk
- 1 tablespoon almond butter

- 1 shallot, thinly sliced
- pinch of dried thyme
- pinch of black pepper
- pinch of sea salt
- 1 tablespoon fat of choice (I used bacon fat)
- coconut oil spray

Bacon Sweet Potato Poutine

PREP TIME: 15 MINUTES • COOK TIME: 25 MINUTES
SERVES: 2

1. Preheat oven to 400°F.
2. Cut the sweet potato in half lengthwise, then slice the sweet potato into 1/2 inch strips, then cut those in half. This is all in an attempt to create the perfect little French fry.
3. Place parchment paper on a baking sheet and place sweet potatoes on it so they are not overlapping.
4. I used coconut oil spray to lightly spray the sweet potatoes then top them with a pinch of salt.
5. Remove the stem from the cauliflower and roughly chop cauliflower into small florets. Cheese curd size will do.
6. Place in a glass baking dish and drizzle a tablespoon or so of your fat of choice.
7. Place cauliflower as well as sweet potatoes in the oven to cook for 20-25 minutes (your cauliflower may take a bit longer).
8. While the goodies are in the oven, add the diced bacon into a skillet over medium heat. Use a wooden spoon to break up the bacon and cook it on all sides.
9. Once bacon is done cooking, remove skillet from heat, take out bacon with a slotted spoon and place on a paper towel.
10. Pour excess bacon fat into a jar or can (save it, ya dummy) leaving 2 tablespoons behind in the skillet for the gravy.
11. Place skillet back over low heat, add the coconut milk and almond butter, then some thyme and black pepper.
12. Let the coconut milk come to a slight boil, then use a spoon to mix together and begin to cook down.
13. Once the mixture begins to thicken, add the bacon back to the gravy and remove from heat.
14. Once the sweet potatoes and cauliflower are done cooking, place in a bowl or on a plate, top with gravy, and devour.

What changes did you make?

_____

_____

_____

REAL IMPORTANT STUFF...
Kind of:

- *This recipe was inspired by a reader who said that their favorite non-paleo food was poutine. I was super intrigued since I had never heard of this Canadian dish. But as soon as I found out what it was, I wanted to make my own rendition. Thank you PaleOMG reader, you're the best!*

INGREDIENTS

For the carrot fries:
- 4-5 long carrots, ends cut off, cut into 1/2 inch-wide strips
- 2 tablespoons olive oil
- 1 tablespoon dried parsley
- 1 tablespoon dried rosemary
- salt and pepper, to taste

For the garlic dip:
- 2 heads of garlic
- 1 cup cashews, roasted and unsalted
- 1/4 cup olive oil
- 1 shallot, minced
- juice of 1/2 a lemon
- 1/2 teaspoon hot sauce
- salt, to taste

Herb Carrot Fries with Roasted Garlic Dip

PREP TIME: 10 MINUTES • COOK TIME: 25 MINUTES

SERVES: 2-4

1. We need to make the best fries ever. Carrot fries. So preheat the oven to 425°F and place the carrot fries on a baking sheet, toss with olive oil, then sprinkle with the herbs, salt and pepper. Lay out the carrots so they aren't overcrowded on the baking sheet.

2. You will also need to roast the garlic, so cut off the end of the head of garlic to show the cloves. Sprinkle a bit of olive oil on the head of garlic, then wrap foil around it. Place the foil packet on another baking sheet (or the same one, if you have room).

3. Bake for 15-20 minutes, flip the carrot sticks over, and then bake for another 20 minutes.

4. While the carrot fries and garlic cloves are roasting, add a small skillet over medium heat and add a teaspoon or so of oil and minced shallots. Cook until translucent then remove from heat.

5. When the garlic cloves are roasted, it's time to squeeze them out into your food processor.

6. Add the cashews and begin to pulse to help the cashews break down.

7. As the cashews begin to become more of a paste, add the olive oil, lemon juice, hot sauce, and a bit of salt.

8. Once all ingredients are incorporated, place in a bowl and fold-in the minced sautéed shallots.

9. Dip away. Carrot fries will change your life.

What changes did you make?

_____

_____

_____

REAL IMPORTANT STUFF... *Kind of:*

HOMEMADE
Honey Cinnamon Almond Butter

INGREDIENTS

PREP TIME: 5 MINUTES
SERVES: 2-3

- 1 1/2 cups almonds, roasted and unsalted
- 1/4 cup almond oil
- 2 tablespoons raw honey
- 1 tablespoon cinnamon
- 1 teaspoon vanilla extract
- pinch of salt

1. Place the roasted, unsalted almonds in a food processor and begin to puree.
2. While your food processor is still running, pour in the almond oil.
3. Add in the raw honey, cinnamon, vanilla extract, and a bit of salt.
4. Mix until well-combined and smooth.
5. Eat with anything. An apple, celery, a spoon… your finger. It all works well.

What changes did you make?

_____

_____

_____

REAL IMPORTANT STUFF... *Kind of:*

- *You can make this nut butter with any kind of nut you want! Macadamia, walnut, pecan. Anything will do!*
- *One time, I thought about making a nut butter business. But I'd rather just share those recipes with you all to make. Way easier.*

Smoked Salmon Deviled Eggs

INGREDIENTS

PREP TIME: 10 MINUTES • COOK TIME: 18 MINUTES

SERVES: 8-12

- 4-6 ounces smoked salmon, cut into 2 inch pieces
- 8-12 eggs
- 1 avocado, pitted
- 2 teaspoons hot sauce
- 1 garlic clove, minced
- 1/2 teaspoon onion powder
- salt and pepper, to taste

1. Place all of the eggs in a saucepan, pour in water to cover eggs, then boil for 15-18 minutes.
2. Place eggs in the fridge to cool.
3. Once eggs have cooled, peel them, cut them in half and remove the yolk. Place all yolks in a food processor, along with the avocado, minced garlic, onion powder, salt and pepper, and puree until smooth.
4. Place the egg-white halves on a plate, top with a square of smoked salmon and push into the egg, and place a spoonful of the egg yolk mixture on the egg.
5. Serve to your happy guests!

What changes did you make?

_____

_____

_____

REAL IMPORTANT STUFF...
Kind of:

- *No smoked salmon? Try mixing some canned salmon, tuna, or even crab into your egg yolk and avocado mixture.*
- *I just gave you a recipe that you can take to parties and make you AND your guests happy! Hallelujah.*

Cuban Turkey Roll-Ups

PREP TIME: 10 MINUTES
SERVES: 2-4

- 4 slices of turkey (sugar, hormone, and nitrate free)
- 4 dill pickles, cut into 1/2 inch-wide strips
- 8 strips of bacon
- 2-3 tablespoons yellow mustard

1. These are super simple to make. You can either bake the bacon, or cook it on a stovetop.
2. I took the stovetop route. Place the bacon in a large skillet and cook on both sides until crispy.
3. Place bacon on a plate covered with a paper towel to soak up the excess fat.
4. Once bacon has cooled a bit, lay out four pieces of turkey.
5. Add a bit of yellow mustard, a couple strips of pickle, and 2 strips of bacon.
6. Roll up the turkey around that goodness and cut in half.

What changes did you make?

_____

_____

_____

REAL IMPORTANT STUFF... *Kind of.*

- Ever had a Cuban sandwich? I haven't. But I've read about them and thought this little turkey roll up would be a good variation.
- I want a Cuban sandwich.

Pumpkin Pie Apple Dip

PREP TIME: 10 MINUTES • COOK TIME: 10 MINUTES

SERVES: 2-4

- 1 (14 ounce) can of pumpkin puree
- 1/2 cup coconut butter, melted
- 3 tablespoons raw honey
- 2 tablespoons canned coconut milk
- 1 teaspoon maple syrup
- 1 teaspoon vanilla extract
- 1 tablespoon cinnamon
- 1/2 teaspoon nutmeg
- 1/4 teaspoon ground cloves
- 1/4 teaspoon ground ginger

1. Place all ingredients in a food processor.
2. Puree.
3. Put into a bowl and serve with apples. Lovely, just lovely.

What changes did you make?

_____

_____

_____

REAL IMPORTANT STUFF... *Kind of:*

- *This is like a dessert holiday dip that you can eat all year round. With any kind of fruit. Or on a paleo muffin. Or on a slice of my blueberry pumpkin loaf. Now I'm just getting crazy.*

149

Desserts

JB's Viewpoint on Paleo Desserts:

Let's talk about sweets people. Holy poo, I love sweets. Like LOVE them. I grew up on peanut butter and chocolate chip sandwiches and swiss rolls in elementary school. Then fell in love with chocolate chip pancakes as my after school snack in high school. Then found out how amazing a two-gallon tub of ice cream and sugar cookie dough can be while studying at my best girlfriend's house in college. Yeah, I'm into sweets. Slightly embarrassing.

But here's the gist. I gain weight VERY easily. Like stupid easily. My metabolism is dumb. So when I eat any sort of sugar, my body goes wild. I can feel the changes that have occurred within hours. And know that the sugar I consumed WILL change my body, and not for the best.

BUT, I'm a human being. A human being who loves sweets. So in no way am I ever going to give them up completely. If I tell myself I can't have something, I want it more. So I have to figure out a solution to my sweets addiction. I can either consume a Cinnabon (holy balls those are good) or I can consume paleo coffee cake. I can consume stuffed French toast from Ihop or I can consume my paleo French toast. So I think this over. What's going to make me feel worse? Grains, or nuts and coconut? Well, my body doesn't like grains. And I probably wouldn't poo for a week if I ate the stuffed French toast from Ihop. So I go with my own version of French toast.

HERE'S WHAT'S ON THE

Menu

Desserts that will make your jaw drop and make you want to eat paleo forever. FOREVER!

COCONUT BITES

CARAMEL CHEESECAKE BARS

DOUBLE DECKER CARROT CAKE CUPCAKES

CHOCOLATE COFFEE CARAMEL BARS

NO BAKE STICKY APPLE BARS

SWEET POTATO BROWNIES WITH VANILLA BEAN ICE CREAM

CHOCOLATE COCONUT BARK

NO BAKE STICKY BERRY BARS

PUMPKIN FREEZER FUDGE

And don't feel sick, I don't feel uncomfortable, and I don't have any regret about what I ate. Makes sense to me.

If I want something sweet, I will eat something that has been paleo-fied and serves the purpose of satisfying my sweets needs. I will stuff the sh*t out of dates with some almond butter and I will be a happy clam. And that's why I love creating my own paleo desserts. I can live a lifestyle that is, well, livable. I can find different options out there that make me happy and don't make me feel like I'm missing out. And that is the key to a healthy diet: having unlimited options to keep you on track. That's why I blog recipes daily and have created this cookbook. To give you all options.

But what I do want to specify, because I have dealt with this issue myself, is that just because it is "paleo" does not mean it is completely good for you. Just like regular desserts, paleo desserts need to be eaten in moderation as well. If your body is like mine, it's not going to love having an entire jar of almond butter or an entire plate of sweet potato brownies. The dimples on my ass increase when the jar of almond butter disappears. It's just plain fact.

So I definitely have to eat in moderation. And control myself, which is always a difficult feat. So when I make these desserts, I'm often taking them to friends. I get to satisfy my sweet tooth and share new recipes with you, while making others happy and helping them find out how amazing the paleo diet can be. That's pretty awesome.

Let's sum this up.

I love sweets. So I eat them in ways that are better FOR ME. That does not mean I think they are extremely healthy and should be consumed daily.

Even though I talk about my love for sweets, when CrossFit competitions come up, my diet changes immensely and I have to eat differently than I did before. That means no dark chocolate for JB. No late light food binges with the bulk aisle.

The inside of a Cinnabon cinnamon roll is tear worthy. True beauty right there. But I must shove that to the back of mind so I can have a digestive tract that works correctly.

So now it's time for you to figure out what works for you. Are you the type that can't have any sweets? Or the type that needs something sweet daily? I don't care either way, just find what works for you. And stop worrying about what others are eating. Having a dessert two or three times a week is what makes me happy. So that's what I do to keep myself sane and smiley. Like sticky apple bars. Those things were awesome. And I made them because I was craving apple pie. It worked. Not craving it anymore. Boom.

Life is all about decisions. The decision to eat something that makes us sick or something that makes us thrive, both physically and mentally. Sticky apple bars make me healthy in the mind. And that's why I love paleo desserts.

Chocolate Coconut Cups

PREP TIME: 10 MINUTES • FREEZE TIME: 20 MINUTES
SERVES: 10-20

- 1 1/2 cups unsweetened shredded coconut
- 1/2 cup coconut butter
- 1/2 cup coconut oil
- 1 teaspoon vanilla extract
- pinch of salt
- 1 bag (10 ounces) of dark chocolate chips

1. Place shredded coconut, coconut butter, coconut oil, vanilla, and salt into a food processor and blend until you get a slightly chunky texture.

2. Place silicone liners into your muffin tin. If you don't have silicone liners, use regular paper muffin liners. If you want to know where to find silicone liners, Google it.

3. Use a large spoon to scoop out about 2 tablespoons worth of coconut mixture and place into your muffin tins. Press down until flat. Fill all liners with the batter.

4. Melt the chocolate. Either place chocolate into a bowl and into the microwave to heat for 30 seconds, then stir, and repeat until chocolate is melted but not burnt. OR use a double boiler to melt down the chocolate. Microwave is easier for lazy people, like yours truly.

5. Use a spoon once again to scoop out about 1 tablespoon of chocolate and pour onto a coconut cup until the coconut is completely covered. Repeat on all the coconut cups.

6. Place in freezer for about 20 minutes or until chocolate is frozen.

7. These will be very hard so you may need to let one sit for a couple minutes at room temperature before biting in. Or break your tooth. Whatever suits your fancy.

8. Keep in fridge or freezer to prevent chocolate from melting.

9. Eat and be merry.

What changes did you make?

_____

_____

_____

REAL IMPORTANT STUFF... *Kind of:*

- *Ever had a Klondike bar? It's kind of like that. But way more awesome.*
- *Add mint to make it more like a mint candy bar. I LOVE CANDY BARS!*

No-Bake Sticky Apple Bars

PREP TIME: 10 MINUTES • FRIDGE TIME: 45 MINUTES
SERVES: 4-6

For the crust:
- 12 medjool dates, pits removed
- 1 cup almond butter
- 1/4 cup raw honey
- 1/4 cup unsweetened shredded coconut
- 1/2 cup coconut butter
- 1 teaspoon cinnamon
- pinch of salt

For the toppings:
- 3 apples, cored and thinly sliced
- 3 tablespoons coconut oil
- 1/2 cup walnuts, roughly chopped
- 1/4 cup raw honey
- 2 tablespoons coconut butter
- pinch of cinnamon
- pinch of salt

1. Make the crust. Add all ingredients for the crust to a food processor (you may need to heat up the coconut butter to melt it down a bit).
2. Put crust ingredients in an 8x8 or 9x9 glass baking dish, press down until evenly distributed.
3. Heat up a large skillet over medium heat. Add the coconut oil then the sliced apples.
4. Once apples begin to soften, add the walnuts. Be sure to continuously stir so the apples and walnuts do not burn.
5. Once apples are wilted, add the honey and coconut butter along with cinnamon and salt.
6. When all ingredients are incorporated, pour mixture on top of crust and press flat. Put in the fridge to harden for 30-45 minutes.
7. Cut into squares and serve!!

What changes did you make?

_____

_____

_____

REAL IMPORTANT STUFF...
Kind of:

- *Ian, the wonderful photographer who took all the awkward photos of me, said these bars were the best things that he's ever tasted. No lie.*
- *These guys can get a little soft and will melt if they are not in the fridge or freezer. Be sure to store them in a cold place before serving!*

For the crust:
- 1 cup almond butter
- 1 cup unsweetened shredded coconut
- 2/3 cup walnuts
- 1 heaping tablespoon coconut butter
- 1 heaping tablespoon raw honey
- pinch of salt

For the filling:
- 1 1/2 cups cashews, roasted and unsalted
- 1/2 cup coconut oil
- 1/2 cup raw honey
- 2-3 tablespoons lemon juice
- 2-4 tablespoons canned coconut milk
- 1 teaspoon vanilla extract

For the caramel:
- 12-14 medjool dates, pitted and soaked in water for an hour
- 5-6 tablespoons canned coconut milk
- 3 tablespoons water
- 1 teaspoon vanilla extract
- pinch of salt
- course sea salt to top it all off with

Caramel Cheesecake Bars

PREP TIME: 30 MINUTES • FREEZE TIME: 1.5-2 HOURS
SERVES: 6-8

1. Place dates in a bowl of water to soak.
2. Let's first make the crust!! Add walnuts to your food processor and blend until you get a meal/flour, almost a walnut butter. Then add the rest of the crust ingredients and blend until well combined.
3. Add crust mixture to an 8x8 glass baking dish lined with plastic wrap, press down until evenly distributed. I sound so professional right now.
4. Wipe out the inside of your food processor, no need to scrub, then add the cashews and blend until you begin to get a clumpy mess.
5. Add the coconut oil, lemon juice, vanilla extract and honey and puree until well combined.
6. Add the coconut milk, 1 tablespoon at a time, and continue to puree to break down the cashews completely. I used about 3 tablespoons for mine until the cashews became a soupy paste.
7. Pour the filling onto the crust and use a knife or spoon to spread mixture throughout the entire pan, covering the crust, then place in the freezer for about 1-2 hours or until completely hard.
8. Once the dates have soaked for about an hour, remove them from the water, and add them to a food processor and pulse until dates have broken down (less than a minute).
9. Add the coconut milk, tablespoon by tablespoon, to the dates while the food processor is still running. Then add the water as well.
10. And add the vanilla extract and pinch of salt.
11. Process until you get a caramel. Just let it run for a while. Pick your nose. Look at a trash magazine and BOOM. Caramel. May take 3-5 minutes, tops. You want it real smooth.
12. Spread caramel over hardened cheesecake filling.
13. Top with some course salt.
14. Place it in the freezer for about 30 minutes until everything has set.
15. Cut bars into the sizes you want. The plastic wrap will help you pull them out without destroying their gorgeous looks. Just pull on the side of the saran wrap and it will pop right out.
16. Eat. Eat and remember how wonderful it is to be paleo.
17. PALEO IS AWESOME!

{ *What changes did you make?*

_____

_____

_____

REAL IMPORTANT STUFF... *Kind of:*

- *You will be amazed how similar this tastes to real cheesecake. I couldn't believe it. So much that I had to sample it many times... until the entire pan was gone. Oops.*
- *No dates on hand to make caramel? Make a fruit jam spread to put on top! Strawberry cheesecake right there!*

INGREDIENTS

For the crust:
- 3 large carrots, shredded (about 1 1/2 cups worth)
- 1 cup almond flour/meal
- 2 eggs, whisked
- 1/4 cup coconut oil, melted
- 1 tablespoon raw honey
- 1 tablespoon cinnamon
- 1 teaspoon vanilla extract
- 1 teaspoon nutmeg
- 1/2 teaspoon ginger
- 1/4 teaspoon cloves
- 1/2 teaspoon baking soda
- 1/2 teaspoon baking powder
- pinch of salt
- 1/4 cup chopped walnuts (optional)
- 1/4 cup raisins (optional)

For the frosting:
- 1 1/2 cups raw cashews (unsalted)
- 5 tablespoons coconut butter
- 1/3 cup canned coconut milk
- 1 tablespoon raw honey
- 2 teaspoons vanilla
- 1/2 teaspoon cinnamon
- pinch of salt

Double Decker Carrot Cake Cupcakes

PREP TIME: 10 MINUTES • COOK TIME: 20 MINUTES

SERVES: 10-12

1. Preheat oven to 350°F.
2. Shred the carrots in your food processor with the shredding attachment or use a grater.
3. Add all the carrot cupcake ingredients to a large bowl and mix thoroughly to combine.
4. Place cupcake ingredients into a silicone or paper-lined muffin tin. Should fill 10-12 muffins.
5. Bake for 18-20 minutes.
6. Add the cashews and pulse until you get a chunky meal/flour.
7. Then add 5 tablespoons of coconut butter.
8. Once that has combined, add coconut milk, honey, vanilla, and cinnamon.
9. When you get a paste/frosting, taste to see if you would like to add any salt.
10. Once the cupcakes are done baking, let cool COMPLETELY, cut in half and place frosting between the two halves, and on top of the cupcake.
11. Sprinkle with cinnamon or extra shredded carrot OR a bit or orange zest!

What changes did you make?

_____

_____

_____

REAL IMPORTANT STUFF... *Kind of:*

- *These don't have to be double decker style. You can just make them like regular cupcakes. I like double decker things though. Like buses.*
- *You could call these carrot cake muffins instead of cupcakes. Then they feel less naughty.*

INGREDIENTS

For the crust:
- 12 dried black figs (or pitted dates, if you prefer), stems removed
- 1/2 cup almond butter
- 1/4 cup unsweetened shredded coconut
- 2 tablespoons raw honey
- 3 tablespoons unsweetened cocoa powder
- 1 teaspoon cinnamon
- pinch of salt

For the caramel:
- 12-14 medjool dates, pitted and soaked in water for an hour
- 5-6 tablespoons canned coconut milk
- 3 tablespoons water
- 1 teaspoon vanilla extract
- pinch of salt

For the topping:
- 1 cup dark chocolate chips, melted
- 1/4 cup canned coconut milk
- 2 teaspoons ground coffee
- pinch of coarse sea salt, to top

Chocolate Coffee Caramel Bars

PREP TIME: 10 MINUTES • FREEZE TIME: 10 MINUTES
SERVES: 5-6

1. Make the crust. Add all of the crust ingredients into a food processor and mix until well combined. Add the crust mixture to a bread pan and push down until the mixture is flat. Like a crust. Duh.

2. Now add the dates and pulse until the dates have broken down (less than a minute). Then add the coconut milk tablespoon by tablespoon to the dates while the food processor is still running. Then add the water as well.

3. And add the vanilla extract and pinch of salt.

4. Process until you get a caramel. BOOM. May take 3-5 minutes, tops.

5. Pour caramel over the crust and spread evenly.

6. Melt the chocolate. You could do this in a double boiler or just the microwave. I chose the latter. I'm lazy.

7. Melt chocolate and coconut milk together in the microwave, heating for 30 seconds then mixing well and reheating if necessary.

8. Once the chocolate is completely melted, add the ground coffee and mix well.

9. Pour melted chocolate over the caramel and spread evenly.

10. Add coarse sea salt on top of the chocolate.

11. Put in freezer to let chocolate harden. Around 10+ minutes.

12. Cut into pieces and eat!!

{

What changes did you make?

_____

_____

_____

REAL IMPORTANT STUFF... *Kind of:*

- *These little bars of heaven in your mouth completely rocked my world. I've even taken them to a potluck in an attempt to make a man fall in love with me. Once again, it didn't work.*
- *No figs on hand? It's cool, just use more of your dates for your crust. But figs are the best dried fruit in the world. Just FYI.*

Sweet Potato Brownies
WITH VANILLA BEAN ICE CREAM

PREP TIME: 35 MINUTES • COOK TIME: 35 MINUTES
SERVES: 5-6

For the brownies:
- 1 sweet potato or yam
- 3 eggs, whisked
- 1/4 cup coconut oil, melted
- 1/3 cup raw honey
- 1/2 cup Enjoy Life Chocolate Chips
- 3 tablespoons coconut flour
- 2 tablespoons unsweetened cocoa powder
- 1/4 teaspoon baking powder
- 1/4 teaspoon vanilla extract
- 1/4 teaspoon cinnamon
- pinch of salt

For the ice cream:
- 2 (14 ounce) cans full fat coconut milk
- 2-3 vanilla beans, slit in half with a knife and remove seeds
- 2 tablespoons raw honey
- 2 teaspoons vanilla extract
- small pinch of salt

To make the brownies:

1. Time to bake that sweet potato. Preheat oven to 425°F, use a fork to add holes all around it, and then throw in the oven for 25-30 minutes. (I'm sure you could micro-wave it, but I like the ole fashioned way. I'm just so ole fashioned).
2. Once the sweet potato is soft and cooked through, peel off the skin and mash it up in a bowl. Turn the oven down to 350°F.
3. Mix together the wet ingredients: coconut oil, honey, vanilla and eggs.
4. Add the dry ingredients: coconut flour, cocoa powder, baking powder, cinnamon, salt and chocolate chips.
5. Mix well to incorporate all that goodness.
6. Pour into an 8x8 glass baking dish.
7. Bake for 30-35 minutes.
8. Let rest to cool a bit.

While the brownies are baking, make the ice cream:

9. Whisk together all ice cream ingredients in a large bowl.
10. Pour into ice cream maker.
11. Let ice cream maker do its thing until the ice cream is frozen.
12. When the brownies have cooled a bit, scoop out the ice cream on top of the brownies and serve. This would look great with a mint leaf, but I ain't that fancy.

What changes did you make?

_____

_____

_____

REAL IMPORTANT STUFF... *Kind of:*

- Think an ice cream maker is a dumb investment? You're wrong.
- If you store these brownies in the freezer, not only will they keep longer, but they become extra chewy. It's awesome.

Chocolate Coconut Bark

PREP TIME: 5 MINUTES • COOK TIME: 45 MINUTES

SERVES: 8+

INGREDIENTS

- 1 cup coconut butter, melted
- 1/2 cup dark chocolate chips
- 1/2 cup unsweetened shredded coconut
- pinch of salt

1. Pull out an 8x8 glass baking dish.
2. Add the chocolate chips to dish and throw in the microwave for about 1:00 (one minute), being sure to mix the chocolate chips if needed to be sure they do not burn. If you are a microwave nazi, use a double boiler to melt the chocolate. It's your chocolate and your world. Do it up.
3. Once chocolate is fully melted, add the coconut butter and shredded coconut and thoroughly mix.
4. Use a spoon to spread mixture out evenly in the baking dish.
5. Top everything off with a sprinkle of salt on top.
6. Put in the freezer for around 45 minutes or more, the use your hands or a knife to chop the bark into pieces.
7. Consume!

What changes did you make?

_____

_____

_____

REAL IMPORTANT STUFF... *Kind of.*

- This is one of the most simple AND most satisfying desserts you'll ever make.
- No 8x8 glass baking dish? That's quite all right! Just place some parchment paper down on a baking sheet and spread your bark out with a spoon. Then it's super easy to break apart!

No Bake Sticky Berry Bars

PREP TIME: 20 MINUTES

SERVES: 5

For the crust:
- 12 medjool dates, pits removed
- 1 cup cashews
- 2 tablespoons almond butter
- 1 teaspoon cinnamon
- pinch of salt

For the toppings:
- 6-8 ounces blackberries
- 6-8 ounces blueberries
- 1/4 cup maple syrup
- 1/4 cup coconut butter
- sprinkle of cinnamon
- pinch of salt

1. Make your crust. Combine all ingredients for the crust in a food processor and pulse.
2. Transfer crust ingredients to a bread pan, and press down until evenly distributed.
3. Heat up a small saucepan under medium heat. Add blackberries and blueberries, along with the maple syrup.
4. Once blueberries and blackberries begin to break down and split (you'll see more juice in the pan), add your syrup. Be sure to continuously stir so the mixture doesn't stick to the bottom or burn.
5. Once you have almost a runny jam, add your melted/softened coconut butter, along with cinnamon and salt.
6. When all ingredients are incorporated, pour mixture on top of crust and press flat. Put in the fridge to harden for 30-45 minutes.
7. Cut into squares and serve!

What changes did you make?

_____

_____

_____

REAL IMPORTANT STUFF... *Kind of:*

- *No blueberries or blackberries? Strawberries and raspberries would be amazing for this!*
- *Want to make these holiday themed? Maybe 4th of July style?! Make half your topping with blueberries and half with strawberries! Wicked cool.*

Pumpkin Freezer Fudge

INGREDIENTS

PREP TIME: 10 MINUTES • FREEZE TIME: 30+ MINUTES

SERVES: 6-8

- 1 cup pumpkin puree
- 1/2 cup almond butter (or other nut/seed butter)
- 1/2 cup coconut oil, melted
- 1/3 cup maple syrup
- 1 tablespoon cinnamon
- 1/2 tablespoon nutmeg
- 1/2 teaspoon ground cloves
- pinch of salt

1. Place all ingredients in a food processor and puree until smooth.
2. Pour mixture into a bread pan and smooth out the top with a spoon.
3. Place in freezer to freeze for 30 minutes or longer. Then cut into fudge-sized pieces. Keep in freezer until you serve. This stuff will melt quickly so only let it thaw for a minute or two before you serve to your guests. Or yourself. You're allowed to be selfish when it comes to fudge.

What changes did you make?

_____

_____

_____

REAL IMPORTANT STUFF... *Kind of:*

- *If this doesn't have holiday dessert written all over it, I don't know what does. Other than every other dessert on this list.*
- *This isn't overly sugary so if you want that sort of thing, add more maple syrup and/or raw honey to the mix.*

Resources

If you want to spice up your meals and find some awesome authors and bloggers out there, here are some resources for you!

Websites to help you understand why paleo is so good for you:
  Robbwolf.com
  Marksdailyapple.com

Food blogs that will help your life never be boring. Support your bloggers!
  Thefoodee.com
  Chowstalker.com
  Desserstalker.com
  Punchfork.com
  Civilizedcaveman.com
  Health-bent.com
  Multiplydelicious.com
  Theclothesmakethegirl.com
  Elanaspantry.com
  Nomnompaleo.com
  Whole9.com
  Primal-palate.com
  Againstallgrain.com
  Urbanposer.com
  Everydaypaleo.com

These books are more than just cookbooks:
  The Paleo Solution by Robb Wolf
  Paleo Comfort Foods by Julie Sullivan Mayfield, Charles Mayfield, Mark Adams and Robb Wolf
  It Starts with Food by Melissa and Dallas Hartwig
  Primal Blueprint by Mark Sisson
  Well Fed by Melissa Joulwan
  Make it Paleo by Bill Staley and Hayley Mason
  Everyday Paleo by Sarah Fragroso
  Practical Paleo by Diane Sanfilippo, Bill Staley and Robb Wolf
  The Gluten-Free Almond Flour Cookbook by Elana Amsterdam

Index

Sweet Potatoes/Yams

Tomatoes

Turkey

Walnuts

Vinegar

Yams/Sweet Potatoes

CPSIA information can be obtained at www.ICGtesting.com
Printed in the USA
LVOW02s1425281013

358940LV00013B/38/P